VIKING WEAPONS
AND
COMBAT TECHNIQUES

VIKING WEAPONS
AND
COMBAT TECHNIQUES

William R. Short

WESTHOLME
Yardley

Frontispiece: Two reenactors demonstrate the combat techniques of the Vikings. (*Photo: Karl Wurst*)

First Westholme paperback September 2014
© 2009 William R. Short

Westholme Publishing, LLC
904 Edgewood Road
Yardley, Pennsylvania 19067
Visit our Web site at www.westholmepublishing.com

ISBN: 978-1-59416-217-6
Also available as an eBook.

Printed in United States of America

Contents

A leaf from Flateyjarbók, perhaps the most beautiful of the medieval Icelandic manuscripts. Stories of Viking-age combat are told in the Icelandic sagas, which are preserved in similar manuscripts. (GkS 1005 fol. 79r, *Stofnun Árna Magnússonar í íslenskum fræðum. Reykjavík*)

INTRODUCTION

THE story of Viking weapons and their use is best told by the *Sagas of Icelanders*: exciting, action-packed stories set in Iceland and other northern lands during the Viking age. The sagas paint clear, compelling pictures of the use of weapons in Viking raids, duels, feuds, and battles:

Thorgeir Starkadarson ran at Gunnar in great anger and thrust his spear through the shield and through Gunnar's arm. Gunnar twisted the shield so hard that the spear broke apart at the socket. Gunnar saw another man come within reach of his sword and struck him his death blow and then seized the halberd in both hands. Thorgeir Otkelsson had meanwhile moved in close, with his sword at the ready. Gunnar turned toward him quickly and in great anger. He thrust his halberd through him and lifted him up high and threw him out into the river. The body drifted down to the ford and was stopped there by a boulder.[1]

The sagas also describe the warriors of the Viking age and the qualities that made them such effective fighters:

Gunnar Hamundarson lived at Hlidarendi in Fljothlid. He was big and strong and an excellent fighter. He could swing a sword and throw a spear with either hand, if he wished, and he was so swift with a sword that there seemed to be three in the air at once. He could shoot with a bow better than anyone else, and he always hit what he aimed at. He could jump higher than his own height, in full fighting gear, and just as far backward as forward.[2]

Despite our having these exciting and compelling narrative descriptions as sources, however, we know comparatively little about Viking-age arms and armor, as compared to weapons from other historical periods. We know even less about how the weapons were used. The surviving records are sparse and contradictory.

This book provides an introduction to the arms and armor of the Vikings, the people who lived in northern Europe during the Viking age (roughly the years 793-1066 C.E.). In addition to describing the weapons, the text puts them in context, showing the place of weapons in Viking society and in the daily lives of the people of the Viking age.

In the book, I first provide an overview of Viking history and culture, focusing on the importance of weapons in the society. Next, I discuss the historical sources available for our research today. I summarize what is known about the defensive and offensive weapons of the Viking age, and then I present our reconstruction of the fighting techniques for Viking sword and shield. I conclude with a summary of what happened to the Vikings after the end of the Viking era.

As will be shown in the text, it is not known how Vikings used their weapons. Relying on a variety of available sources, I and my colleagues

---

1. Robert Cook, tr. Njal's Saga, from *The Complete Sagas of the Icelanders*, Viðar Hreinsson, ed. (Reykjavík: Bókútgáfan Leifur Eiríksson hf., 1997.) vol. 3, ch. 72, p. 84.

2. Ibid., ch.19, p. 24.

at Hurstwic (a Viking-age living history organization) and at the Higgins Armory Sword Guild (an organization that researches and practices historical European martial arts) have begun to reconstruct the lost combat techniques of the Viking age.

This reconstruction is highly speculative, due to the paucity of hard evidence, but the techniques are based on a variety of historical sources including the combat treatises that survive from Europe's Middle Ages.

The Viking people had a lasting impact on Europe through their voyages of trade and exploration. Today, the Viking culture continues to hold the popular imagination in media ranging from comic strips to feature films to computer games. In this text, I also hope to set straight some popular misconceptions about Viking warriors and their use of weapons that continue to thrive in these fantasy sources.

Throughout the book, I draw heavily on examples from *Sagas of Icelanders*. Although the sagas have few specific combat details, the stories are invaluable. They are stories set in the Viking age written by authors familiar with and experienced in the use of weapons for an audience that, likewise, was familiar with and experienced in the use of weapons. They describe how these weapons were used, not by kings or heroes or gods or trolls, but by ordinary men as part of their everyday lives.

Because I quote frequently from the sagas in the text, I use many Icelandic names and words. In the Viking age, the northern people spoke the same language, which they called *dönsk tunga* (the Danish tongue), and which we now call common Scandinavian or old Norse. Modern Scandinavian languages are direct descendants, and modern English, German, and Dutch are cousins.

By the time the sagas were written down, the Scandinavian languages had started to diverge from one another. The language of the sagas is called old Icelandic. Modern Icelandic has remained close to the language of the sagas, in part because the Icelanders never stopped reading their medieval sagas. Whenever the Icelandic language started to drift, language reforms were instituted to bring it back to align with the language of the sagas.

Compared to the English language, Icelandic has two additional consonants in the alphabet: þ (thorn) pronounced like the "th" in *Thor*; and ð (edh) pronounced like the "th" in *father*.

Icelandic has many more vowel sounds than does English, resulting in accents (such as *â*), ligatures (such as *æ*), and umlauts (such as *ö*) being used to represent the additional sounds. Readers are welcome to pronounce these as they please because there are no English equivalents.

In the text, I've followed the spelling conventions of *Íslenzk fornrit*, the standard scholarly edition of the sagas. I have tried to render Icelandic names in normalized old Icelandic in the nominative case, although I realize that I have not been completely consistent in my efforts. I use the English possessive "'s" throughout rather than the Icelandic possessive form (genitive). So when I write about the sword owned by Björn, I write *Björn's sword*, and not *Bjarnar*, as it would be written in Icelandic.

The Viking people did not use last names or family names, a practice that is still widely followed in modern Iceland. Instead, infants were given names that were used in combination with a patronymic. For example, in *Egils saga Skalla-Grímssonar*, Egill Skalla-Grímsson (Egill, son of Skalla-Grímr) took as his wife Ásgerðr Bjarnardóttir (Ásgerðr, daughter of Björn). Ásgerðr's name did not change after her marriage; she retained her patronymic name. Among their children were Böðvarr Egilsson (son of Egill) and þorgerðr Egilsdóttir (daughter of Egill).

Some people earned nicknames. *Landnámabók*, a history of the settlement of Iceland, is filled with examples for which the meaning of the nickname is clear: Helgi enn magri (the lean); Eiríkr rauði (the red), Ljótr enn spaki (the wise); and Auðr en djúpauðga (the deep minded). However, one has to wonder how þorgrímr tordýfill (dungbeetle) earned his nickname.

In the text, I've tried to uniquely identify each saga character with a name and either patronymic or nickname, when they are so identified in the saga. Some characters are so minor that only their given name is used in the sagas, and thus, in this text as well.

I have left place names in the Icelandic, rather than translating them. So, I use *Smjörvatnsheiði* rather than *Butter Lake Heath*.

Throughout the text, I occasionally use terminology that is specific to the practice of European martial arts of the Middle Ages and that may be unfamiliar to the reader. I try to define the terms when first using them.

For example, one such frequently used term is *line of attack*, which is simply the planned trajectory of the weapon to its target. For a given target on the body, there are many possible lines of attack. As is discussed in detail later, one benefit of a large Viking shield is that it closes, or blocks, many lines of attack simultaneously, limiting the possible sites an opponent can target.

In the descriptions of the combat techniques, I often use *combatant* and *opponent* to describe the two fighters. Typically, *combatant* refers to the person initiating the attack, and *opponent* refers to the person responding to and defending against the attack.

Because virtually all Viking weapons were made from iron, the text often mentions iron and its various alloys, such as steel. To avoid being swamped by the complexities of the metallurgy of Viking weapons, I tend to use the word *iron* to mean all forms of iron and its alloys. In a few cases where steel was used for Viking weapons, I specifically call out that form of iron.

The Battle of Stamford Bridge took place in the year 1066, and is commonly taken as the end of the Viking age. (*P. N. Arno, Slaget ved Standford Bridge, 1870, photo © O. Væring Eftf. AS*)

1

Overview of Weapons in Viking-Age Society

Weapons were a part of everyday life in the Viking age. Virtually every free man owned and carried a weapon and was familiar and comfortable with its use. The right to carry and use weapons was one of the fundamental rights of free men in Viking society. That right was limited only to free men; women and slaves did not typically carry or use weapons.

Throughout this book, I, like most people, use the term *Viking* incorrectly. To the people whom we moderns call *Vikings*, that word implied an activity, and the individuals who participated in that activity.

Today, we would call that activity *raiding*. The old Icelandic word for this activity, *víking*, didn't imply a culture, or a time, or a land to these people, as it does in modern usage. Regardless, in this book, I, like many authors before me, employ the inaccurate but widely accepted modern usage and refer to Viking people and Viking lands and Viking times.

The Viking age is often arbitrarily defined to be the period between the years 793 and 1066. In 793, heathen sea raiders plundered the monastery at Lindisfarne off the northeast coast of England, the first recorded Viking raid. In 1066, King Haraldr harðráði (hard-ruler) of Norway was repulsed by King Harold Godwinsson of England in the Battle of Stamford Bridge, the last major Viking raid.

Not only is the Viking age defined by the raids in modern usage, but the Viking people often are, too. That definition is inaccurate in several ways.

Many Europeans, other than Vikings, participated in this kind of raiding during this period in history. Vikings were scarcely the only raiders taking advantage of the chaotic political situation in Europe, and of the shifting trade routes and trade centers that brought more of the world's wealth within their reach.

The Vikings, however, are better remembered for raiding than their contemporaries for several reasons. Their raids were more successful and more far ranging than those of other Europeans, due to the superiority of the their ships. That they were heathen marauders defiling Christian churches made them especially abhorrent to the historians of the time, who were virtually all Christians. As a result, the Vikings got a lot of bad press in the contemporary histories: "filthy pestilence," "unspeakable evil," and "a most vile people." Yet contemporary histories paint varying portraits of the Viking raiders, compared to the other raiders of that era.

On one hand, some contemporary histories suggest that Vikings were less destructive than other raiders. Vikings were entrepreneurs looking to turn a profit. They wanted easy loot that

A Viking mêlée is recreated by modern reenactors.

could be conveniently carried away. They were not much interested in mass killings, or sacking towns, or destroying harvests. Vikings tended not to destroy buildings, as did other raiders; they merely took all the valuable fittings. Vikings didn't destroy the vineyards at Aquitaine, the way the Frankish raiders did. Vikings were more interested in taking prisoners that could be ransomed or sold as slaves, rather than in killing them or violating them. There are examples of Frankish women taking refuge with the Viking raiders, apparently expecting to find greater safety there than with other raiders.

On the other hand, some contemporary histories are filled with overwrought descriptions of heathen Viking invaders ravaging everything in their path with their acts of burning, looting, devastation, rape, and sacrilege. It is this view that colors modern popular opinions about Vikings and their activities.

Recent scholarly research takes a more measured assessment of the Vikings' activities. Although they did their part to disrupt the regions along Europe's coast and inland water-

ways, they did not mindlessly destroy everything and kill everyone in their path. More likely, they exhibited no worse behavior, and possibly some better, than the other European raiders during the Viking age. The activities of the Vikings were no more or less odious than those of other raiders, but because the Vikings were heathens when the rest of Europe was primarily Christian, their activities were taken to be sacrilegious, and thus exceptionally offensive to the educated clergy who were writing the contemporary histories.

A better definition of the word *Viking* might be that the Vikings were those people who lived in the Scandinavian lands (Denmark, Norway, and Sweden), and their North Atlantic settlements (Iceland, Greenland, the Faroe Islands, and others) during the Viking age. These northern people shared a common culture. For much of the Viking age, these people from Greenland to the Baltic spoke the same language, used the same alphabet, worshipped the same gods, and adopted the same styles of fashion and adornment, with only slight variations from land to land.

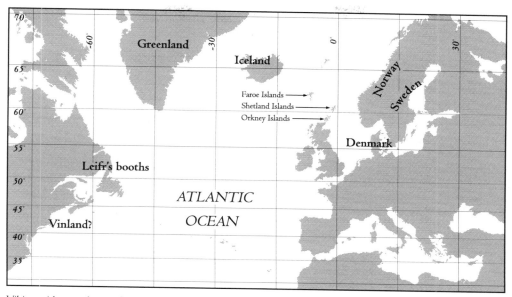

Viking raiders, traders, and explorers reached virtually all of the lands shown on this map. Their Scandinavian homelands and North Atlantic settlements are labeled.

During the Viking age, these people traveled outside of their homelands to every corner of the known world: to the east coast of North America; throughout continental Europe; through the lands around the Mediterranean including Africa and Jerusalem; and across Russia to the Black Sea and Caspian Sea.

However, few of these people actually participated in raiding. In the Viking age, everyone had to grow their own food, so everyone was first a farmer. There were few professional soldiers or professional raiders, especially in the early part of the Viking age. People lived on farms and grew the food and manufactured the tools, clothing, and other materials they needed for their daily lives.

Some farmers were also part-time blacksmiths, or carpenters, or traders. A few farmers might choose to be part-time raiders: Vikings. It was the kind of adventure that was desirable for a young man to prove himself, but a more mature man was expected to settle down on the farm and raise a family.

Ketill Ormsson expressed this view to his son in chapter 2 of *Vatnsdæla saga*, thought to have been written near the beginning of the fourteenth century. He was not pleased that his son had taken no initiative in rooting out a highwayman working nearby who had killed dozens of travelers. Ketill rebuked the young man, saying,

The ways of young people today aren't what they were when I was young. Back then, young men were eager to do some notable deed, either taking part in a raid, or gaining wealth and honor in expeditions that called for manliness. But nowadays, young people prefer to be stay-at-homes, sitting at the kitchen fire and filling their bellies with mead and small-beer.

Ketill concluded by advising his son, "You have now reached the age when it would be right for you to put yourself to the test and find out what fate has in store for you."

As Ketill told his son, raiding brought honor and wealth, the two qualities a man needed to advance in Viking society.

The Norse myths say that at the birth of every child, the three Norns, the women of destiny, set the moment for the child's death. (*detail from J. L. Lund, De tre norner, 1844, Statens Museum for Kunst*)

In the mind of the Viking people, raiding was very distinct from theft. Theft was abhorrent, whereas raiding was an honorable challenge to a fight, with the victor earning the spoils in reward for his martial prowess. The distinction is vividly evoked in chapter 46 of the *Egils saga*. While raiding a coastal farm on the Baltic Sea, Egill Skalla-Grímsson and his men were captured by the farmer and his family, who bound up the raiders. During the night, Egill managed to slip his bonds. He and his men grabbed their captors' treasure and headed back to their ship. Along the way, Egill was struck with remorse: "This journey is terrible and hardly suitable for a warrior. We have stolen the farmer's money without his knowledge. We should never allow such shame to befall us." Egill returned to the farmer's house, set it ablaze, and killed the occupants as they tried to escape the smoke and flames. He then returned to his ship with his honor enhanced.

The word *honor* imperfectly expresses the depth and complexity of the concept in the Viking age. *Honor* referred to the social credibility of those who possessed it. A person with honor was not to be trifled with: his reputation

encouraged others to treat him with respect in social, legal, and mercantile interactions. Someone without honor was fair game for the unscrupulous.

Honor had a metaphysical dimension as well. One of the beliefs of the Norse heathen religion was that few people lived on after their death. The afterlife was not a prominent feature of Norse paganism. Thus, the main attributes that survived a man's death were his good name, reputation, and honor. Honor had an enduring value that ranked above any mere physical possession.

For all these reasons, one was expected to defend one's honor against any indignity, no matter how small. It was better to preserve one's honor without the use of arms if possible, but it must be preserved regardless of the cost. *Hávamál*, a poem of ethics and advice from the Viking age, says that one should constantly be on the alert for wrongs and make no peace with one's enemies. A family's honor was a tribute to its ancestors and a legacy for its descendants, and so people were obligated to preserve their honor and enrich it if possible so that their entire kin group benefited. To possess honor was a significant practical asset in every kind of transaction in the Viking age.

Another aspect of the Viking heathen religious beliefs that guided Viking behavior was fate. According to the Norse myths, the three Norns chose the time of a man's death on the day he was born. No man outlived the night that the Norns decreed for his death.

Even though the moment of death was preordained, however, nothing else in life was. Therefore, a person living in the Viking age would have every reason to be bold. In any venture, the best that could happen was fame and fortune, and the increase in honor that attended a successful fight. The worst that could happen was death, and because of fate, death would occur whether someone stayed home safe in bed, or engaged in a fight against all odds. Therefore, there was no reason to be retiring and every reason to be bold and adventuresome.

This belief is illustrated by an episode in chapter 47 of *Sverris saga*. King Sverrir Sigurðarson addressed his troops before a battle and related a story about a father giving counsel to his young son before a battle:

> A farmer accompanied his son to the warships and gave him advice, telling him to be valiant and hardy in perils. "How would you act if you were engaged in battle and knew beforehand that you were destined to be killed?"
>
> The son answered, "Why then should I refrain from striking right and left?"
>
> The farmer said, "Now suppose someone could tell you for certain that you would not be killed?"
>
> The son answered, "Why then should I refrain from pushing forward to the utmost?"
>
> The farmer said, "In every battle where you are present, one of two things will happen: you will either fall or come away alive. Be bold, therefore, for everything is preordained. Nothing can bring a man to his death if his time has not come, and nothing can save one doomed to die. To die in flight is the worst death of all."

These two forces, fate and honor, drove Vikings to be bold and adventuresome, searching for ways to increase honor, and sensitive to any attempt to diminish honor. The use of weapons was a fundamental part of this bold behavior. One defended one's honor with weapons. One performed bold adventures with weapons.

A *drengr* (honorable man) was brave, honest, fearless, with a sense of fair play, and a respect for others. He always kept his word. Strength, although admired, needed to be moderated so one did not become *ójafnaður* (unjust).

The Alþing, the national parliament of Viking-age Iceland, is shown in session. (*William Collingwood, The Icelandic Thing, 1875, © The Trustees of the British Museum*)

Countless examples from the sagas show the values that were admired: valor, generosity, restraint, moderation, self-control, refusal to indulge in emotional outbursts, sense of humor, imperturbability, stoicism, and the refusal to give way in the face of insurmountable odds.

Hávamál offers further guidance. Value wisdom and common sense. Be thoughtful, sparing of words, cheerful, mindful, and affable. Be independent even if it means owning few possessions. Be decent but not overly concerned about appearance. Have reasonable ambitions, neither too great nor too modest. Be a friend to a friend, and repay gift with gift. Value friendship most of all. For a friend, no sacrifice is too great. For an enemy, no scruples need be observed.

Additionally, the governmental structure in the Viking lands encouraged the use of weapons. Although there were regular parliamentary meetings called *þing* which met to make laws and to judge the laws, there was no executive branch of government to enforce the laws.

There was no army nor any police force. After the court rendered its verdict, it was up to

A Viking-age duel. (*Johannes Flintoe, Havnen i Skiringssal, 1830, Photo © O. Væring Eftf. AS*)

the injured parties and their allies to enforce the judgment of the court, and that enforcement usually involved the use of weapons, or the credible threat of the use of weapons.

Despite this lack of any formal enforcement agency, adherence to the law was highly regarded, as observed by several notable Icelanders in the sagas. Þorgeirr Ljósvetningagoði said, "if we tear apart the law, we tear apart the peace."

We know more about the legal system in Iceland than in other Viking lands because more was written there, in sagas and in law codes. The Icelandic legal system served as a vehicle for managing conflict and violence. Violence was not only regarded as an appropriate way of resolving conflict but was also prescribed by law in some cases. However, Icelanders understood the need to limit that violence so that the fabric of society was not threatened and so that lives were not taken unnecessarily. In the words of *Hávamál*, "It is better to be alive ... a corpse is of no use to anyone."

In Viking-age Iceland, violent conflict was governed by the culture of the feud. The Icelandic blood feud was a stabilizing force that channeled conflict within acceptable limits. In a society without any centralized state authority,

individuals and groups had to rely on their own resources to avoid being victimized by those around them. Any offense that challenged the honor of an individual or family or group had to be met with a deterrent response, a response that included the use of weapons. The blood feud was a system of social conventions that sanctioned private retribution for offenses, while limiting escalation and avoiding broader social damage.

A common sentence for some offenses was outlawry. Someone subject to full outlawry (*skóggangr*) was placed, quite literally, outside the protection of the law. He was banished from society. His property was confiscated. He could not be fed or sheltered. He could be killed without penalty by anyone who saw him. In lesser outlawry (*fjörbaugsgarðr*), the guilty party was banished for only three years. His property was not confiscated, making it possible for him to return to a normal life after three years abroad.

For other offenses, the law specified an appropriate monetary compensation, paid by the guilty party to the injured party. The law provided for standard amounts of compensation, depending on the injury and the status of the parties involved.

Hólmrinn, the dueling site at Þingvellir in Iceland, was probably located in the foreground of the photograph. Lögberg, the rocky outcrop that was the focal point of Þingvellir, is at the top of the hill marked with the flagpole.

Some crimes, particularly crimes that diminished a man's honor, were considered so offensive that immediate, lethal revenge was not only sanctioned by law but also required by societal mores. The law permitted a man who was seriously injured or dishonored to avenge himself without penalty at any time up until the case was brought to court. Although compensation satisfied the need for justice in many instances, there were others where no monetary compensation would restore lost honor. Honorable men refused the shame of carrying money in their purse as compensation for a dead kinsmen.

Revenge need not be worked upon the offender himself. It was equally effective to take vengeance against a closely related family member of equal status. In *Hrafnkels saga Freysgoða*, years after Sámr Bjarnason humiliated Hrafnkell Freysgoði, Hrafnkell began taking his revenge by attacking and killing Sámr's brother Eyvindr Bjarnason, who had just returned home from a seven-year trading voyage, and who had not been a party to any of the disputes between Sámr and Hrafnkell.

Another legally sanctioned way of making good on injuries or settling disputes was the duel. The less formal form of dueling was known as *einvígi* (single combat), whereas the more formal duel was called *hólmganga* (going to the island) because duels were frequently fought on small islands. The islands prevented cowards from running away and limited possible interference from third parties.

The sagas say that many duels in Iceland were fought at Hólmrinn, an island in the Öxará river at Þingvellir, the site of the annual Alþing assembly. The exact location of the island is not known, and the topography of the valley has changed considerably in the centuries since the sagas. However, many believe that a likely location is where several smaller islands are now located in the river, southeast of Lögberg, the law-speaker's rock visible in the photo above.

The difference between the two forms of dueling was significant, as evidenced by an exchange of dialog in chapter 10 of *Kormáks saga*. Kormákr Ögmundarson challenged Bersi Véleifsson to a formal duel. When they met to fight, Bersi offered instead the less formal single combat. "You are a young, inexperienced man. There is difficulty involved in a hólmganga, but none in an einvígi."

Portions of the law code recorded in Grágás, the medieval Icelandic lawbook, are thought to represent the law as practiced in Viking-age Iceland. (*Staðarhólsbók AM 334 fol. 27v, Stofnun Árna Magnússonar í íslenskum fræðum. Reykjavík*)

One has the sense that for an einvígi, men simply met and fought, typically to the death, with few formalities.

Hólmganga, however, had an elaborate set of preparations and customs, and the duel could be ended honorably after first blood. In many sagas in which a hólmganga takes place, the dueling laws (*hólmgöngulög*) are recited. The laws, as they appear in each saga, differ from one instance to another in significant ways. In some cases, they seem too fantastic to be plausible. For example, the dueling laws recited in chapter 10 of *Kormáks saga* describe the preparation of the dueling cloak, which was pegged to the ground and marked the boundaries of the dueling space. The saga says that the person who prepares the pegs that fasten the dueling cloak to the ground must approach the pegs in such a way that he can see the sky between his legs

while grasping his earlobes and speaking an invocation.

Duels had long since ceased to be a common occurrence by the time the sagas were committed to written form, so saga authors may have taken some liberties in reciting the dueling laws. The last hólmganga in Iceland occurred early in the 11th century, between Gunnlaugr ormstunga (serpent tongue) and Hrafn Önundarson. The next day, the Alþing passed a law abolishing duels.

Dishonor could occur at any time an individual was perceived as suffering some injury without exacting retribution. In many cases, the injury might be material: robbery, damage to property, physical injury, or an unjust business deal. The dishonor occurred whether the injury was to oneself, a relative, or a subordinate.

Nonmaterial injuries were equally threatening to honor. Some insults were considered so powerful that, by law, a man was free to kill someone who spoke them. Many of these insults relate to transgressions against gender roles and are among the offenses listed in the *Grágás*, a medieval Icelandic law book. Portions of the law were first written down in 1117, and many of the laws in the *Grágás* are thought to represent those practiced in Iceland during the Viking age. The law says that if a man calls another man womanish, or says that he has been buggered, the recipient of the insult has the right to kill in retaliation.

In chapter 123 of *Brennu-Njáls saga*, Flosi þórðarson, thinking he had been insulted by Njáll þorgeirsson, taunted him, saying, "There are many who can't tell by looking at him whether he is a man or a woman." Njáll's son, Skarpheðinn, responded in kind: "You are the bride of the troll at Svínafell; people say he uses you as a woman every ninth night." Flosi later avenged the insult by burning down Njáll's house at Bergþórshváll, killing Njáll, Skarpheðinn, and many others in the flames.

Insults were thought to be even more powerful when expressed in verse. The penalty for composing even a half a stanza of poetry with defamation or mockery in it was full outlawry.

Dishonor could also be imparted with actions. A variety of activities meant to mock or disgrace a man are described in the stories and law codes and were prohibited by law. Intentionally making someone dirty, tearing or cutting their clothing, or anything meant to disgrace could be punished with full outlawry.

A memorable example is told in chapter 25 of *Reykdæla saga og Víga-Skútu*. Þorgeirr Þórisson wished to avenge the death of his father on Skúta Áskelsson at the Alþing meeting. To get Skúta's attention, Þorgeirr arranged for Skúta's residence at Alþing to be used as a latrine all summer, before the assembly convened. Skúta acknowledged the prank by killing Þorgeirr with a blow from his axe.

Physical symbols could also impart dishonor. In chapter 2 of *Gísla saga Súrssonnar*, Kolbjörn accepted a duel with Hólmgöngu-Skeggi (Skeggi the dueler) over the matter of which of the two would marry Gísli Súrsson's sister, Þórdís Súrsdóttir. Intimidated by Skeggi's reputation, Kolbjörn reneged on his obligation, so Gísli took his place. Skeggi arrived at the dueling site before Gísli and concluded that both men had backed out, a shameful disgrace. Skeggi told a carpenter to make wooden effigies of Gísli and Kolbjörn, one behind the other, to mock and shame them. Although not explicit, a sexual insult is clearly intended.

Given the importance of maintaining honor against even the slightest provocation in Viking society, it is no surprise that weapons were a part of everyday life in the Viking age. A violent attack to restore lost honor could take place at any time against any man, inside and outside the house. The sagas are filled with examples of unexpected violent attacks with lethal intent: an

Men in the Viking age carried their weapons not only while traveling, but also at home while performing their routine everyday activities.

attack over the dinner table (*Bandamanna saga* chapter 4); an attack while seeing a guest off the farm (*Bjarnar saga Hítdælakappa* chapter 19); an attack while sleeping in bed (*Gísla saga* chapter 16); an attack while going out to use the outhouse (*Eyrbyggja saga* chapter 26); an attack while playing *knattleikr*, the Viking ball game (*Egils saga*, chapter 40); an attack while working in the farm fields (*Grettis saga Ásmundarsonar* chapter 48); an attack while in court (*Brennu-Njáls saga* chapter 145).

To be prepared for these kinds of unpredictable attacks, it is highly likely that free men carried their weapons with them routinely.

Hávamál warns that a man should be prepared to fight at any moment, day or night. Verse 38 says you should never step more than one pace away from your weapon because you don't know for certain when you might need it.

The stories suggest that men carried weapons not only while traveling away from

Knattleikr, the Viking ballgame, was played here at the farm of Knörr in west Iceland.

home, but also at home while performing everyday activities.

Chapter 111 of *Brennu-Njáls saga* says that Höskuldr þráinsson carried his weapon with him when he went to work the grain fields at his farm, Ossabær.

After dressing in the morning, Höskuldr took his seed bag in one hand and his sword in the other and left to work his fields. The sons of Njáll were waiting behind the fence and ambushed Höskuldr. His sword didn't help him. Skarpheðinn struck the first blow, and then the rest joined in the killing.

In chapter 48 of *Grettis saga*, þorbjörn Arnórsson and his son Arnórr were working in their hayfield, bundling hay. Arnórr had a wood axe in his hand, and þorbjörn had just set his sword and shield down next to the bundle of hay he was tying when Grettir Ásmundarson arrived. þorbjörn picked up his shield and drew his sword to face Grettir as Arnórr worked his way around to Grettir's back. Grettir killed Arnórr with the backswing of his sax (short sword) and then killed þorbjörn with the downswing.

Atli worked at the farm at þórólfsfell, making charcoal by burning chipped wood from the forest. Chapter 38 of *Brennu-Njáls saga* says that he worked with a spear stuck in the ground by his side. Even that degree of preparedness wasn't sufficient. Brynjólfr, hidden by the smoke from the fire pit, walked right up to Atli and struck him on the head with his axe, causing Atli's death.

Chapter 43 of *Eyrbyggja saga* tells of an attempted killing during the ball games that were played below the mountain Öxl, south of the farm Knörr. It was Björn Ásbrandsson and þórðr blíg's turn to start the fire and fetch the water for the evening meal as the games were winding down for the day.

As they worked, a clumsy assassin named Egill entered the shed, hidden by the smoke of the fire. He tripped over his shoelace and fell headlong into the shed. Björn pounced on him, while þórðr picked up a nearby sword. Even while performing these domestic chores, a weapon was no more than an arm's length away.

Weapons were hung on the wall, over the bed, ready for instant use should an attack occur in the night. The master's bedcloset at the reconstructed Viking-age farmhouse at Stöng is shown on the facing page, with his axe and sword on the wall ready for his immediate use.

Weapons were prized gifts. *Hávamál* says friends should exchange weapons as gifts.

Weapons were given names: Grettir carried the sax *Kársnautr* (Kár's gift), Bolli carried the sword *Fótbítr* (Leg-biter), and Skarpheðinn carried the axe *Rimmugýgr* (Battle-Ogre).

Weapons were an integral part of the society. Free men likely carried a weapon habitually. But the carrying of weapons was limited *only* to free men. Women and the unfree, such as slaves, were prohibited from carrying weapons. There are examples in the stories of slaves and women owning weapons, but the stories and the law-books make it clear that their carrying or using those weapons was neither permitted nor customary. With few exceptions, women's graves do not contain weapons in Viking lands, in the way that men's graves commonly do. Weapons were not a part of the lives of women.

In Viking society, men and women each had distinctive roles to play. In practical terms, the responsibilities for each gender were defined physically by the threshold of the outer door of the house. Men were responsible for the outdoor work: agriculture, animal husbandry, trade, and all the external relations with government and community.

Women were responsible for work inside the house, including child rearing, food preparation and service, and cloth and clothing production. Women took the agricultural products raised by men and turned them into useful items for the family's consumption.

The overall framework was predictably patriarchal, with legal, governmental, and domestic authority concentrated in male hands. A woman was, by law, under the authority of her husband or father. She had only limited freedom to dispose of property belonging to her. She was prohibited from participating in most political or governmental activities. She could not be a chieftain, a judge, or a witness nor could she participate in a legal assembly.

On the other hand, women enjoyed an unusual level of respect and freedom in Viking society, compared to other European societies during the period. Women managed the family finances. Women ran the farm during their husbands' absences. In widowhood, women could be rich and important landowners. The law protected women from a wide range of unwanted attention ranging from kissing to intercourse. Women could declare themselves divorced

Top: Weapons hang on the wall above the bed, ready for instant use, at a reconstruction of the Viking-age farmhouse at Stöng in south Iceland. Bottom: The dividing line between men's responsibilities and women's responsibilities was the threshold of the front door. Men looked outward, to the farm, the community, and external relations, while women looked inward, to family, house, and home.

Women were responsible for the work inside the house. In the hall of the reconstructed Viking-age farm at Eiríksstaðir in west Iceland, two women are surrounded by spinning, weaving, and cooking tools.

through a simple verbal formula recited before witnesses. The sagas often show women playing strong, dynamic roles.

Because of the legal and practical limitations imposed on them, women in the sagas typically achieved power through their ability to influence the actions of the men around them. In chapter 48 of *Laxdæla saga*, Guðrún Ósvífrsdóttir incited her husband Bolli Þorleiksson and her brothers to take revenge on Kjartan Ólafsson, Bolli's beloved foster brother. Knowing that Bolli was repulsed at the thought of such a despicable act, Guðrún used all the manipulative eloquence she could command to put her kinsmen's manhood on the line:

Guðrún is buried here at the farm of Helgafell in west Iceland.

With your temperament, you'd have made some farmer a good group of daughters, fit to do no one any good or any harm. After all the abuse and shame Kjartan has heaped upon you, you don't let it disturb your sleep while he goes riding by your home with only one other man to accompany him. Such men have no better memory than a pig. There's not much chance you will ever dare to make a move against Kjartan at home if you won't even stand up to him now, when he only has one or two others with him. The lot of you just sit at home, making much of yourselves, and one could only wish there were fewer of you.

The scene derives additional poignancy because Guðrún was formerly betrothed to Kjartan, and events in the story suggest that her fury was partly fueled by disappointed love. At the end of the saga, the aged Guðrún, who was four times widowed, was asked by her son which man she most loved.

She cryptically replied, "I was worst to him I loved best."

Guðrún is buried in a grave outside the churchyard at her farm at Helgafell.

Left: A typical Viking-age man was armed with a shield and a single weapon, such as an axe. Right: A more wealthy man might own a more prestigious weapon, such as a sword.

The prohibition against women carrying weapons brought with it some level of protection against violence. It was considered shameful in the extreme to harm a woman, even accidentally, in a fight. That is not to say that such attacks never occurred, but when they did occur, honorable men condemned them and banded together to hunt down the guilty party immediately for his shameful deed. Even mild violence was objectionable. In chapter 10 of *Droplaugarsona saga*, Helgi Droplaugarson chided his men for playfully throwing a snowball at a woman: "Only an idiot attacks a woman."

There are a few examples in the stories where women use weapons. Typically, they do so when their husbands act in a cowardly or shameful manner. In such cases, women may take matters into their own hands, as is told in chapter 37 of *Gísla saga*. After the cowardly Eyjólfr Þórðarson had killed Gísli Súrsson at Geirþjófsfjörðr, he went to the farm at Helgafell to visit Börkr Þorsteinsson, and his wife Þórdís Súrsdóttir, who was Gísli's sister. Börkr welcomed Eyjólfr and invited him to tell the story of the deed. Þórdís wanted to offer only meager hospitality to her brother's killer, but Börkr gave him a warm welcome. After the meal had been served,

Þórdís intentionally dropped a tray full of spoons. As she bent down to pick up the spoons, she saw Gísli's sword lying at Eyjólfr's feet. She grabbed the sword and thrust up at Eyjólfr, intending to run him through, but the crossguard on the sword's hilt caught against the edge of the table. The blade was deflected, and Eyjólfr received only a wound in the thigh. Börkr seized Þórdís and wrenched the sword from her grasp. She declared herself divorced from Börkr on the spot.

ALTHOUGH it is likely that every free man had at least one weapon, it's also likely that few men had more than one. In the Viking age, iron was difficult and time-consuming to create, and thus iron was expensive. Anything requiring a lot of iron in its construction, such as a weapon, was a costly item. Further, some weapons, such as swords, were so difficult to fabricate that only highly specialized smiths could make them, further adding to their value and prestige.

As a result, a typical man was armed with nothing more than a shield and an axe, or perhaps a shield and a spear. A poor man might simply use the wood axe from the farm, if he had nothing else available.

Left: As he accumulated more success and more wealth, a man might acquire additional weapons, such as a sax, and he might replace plain weapons with more ornately decorated ones. Right: Only the extremely wealthy could own the full range of expensive arms and armor shown here: shield, helmet, mail, sword, spear, and axe.

A more wealthy man might own a sword, which in the Viking age, was worth a dozen or more milk cows. Because having just one more milk cow might mean the difference between starving to death and surviving over the winter in the Viking age, a sword was a valuable possession indeed.

A man with more wealth, perhaps someone who returned from successful Viking raids, might replace his ordinary sword and shield with ornate, prestige weapons. Perhaps he might add a second weapon, such as a sax (short sword), to his set of arms.

Only the extremely wealthy, those at the top of the social hierarchy, could afford to own the full panoply of weapons and defenses shown here: axe, spear, mail, helmet, along with sword and shield. Such displays of wealth must have been rare in the Viking age.

A study of Viking-age burials in western Norway revealed that of the graves in which weapons were found, 61 percent of them contained one weapon, while only 15 percent contained three or more.

Throughout these pages, I have used images of historical weapons and modern reproductions based on historical examples. To avoid confusion, each is clearly identified in the text. I've used images of modern reproductions extensively, in part, because the appearance of the historical weapons has often degraded significantly over the centuries, due to their excavated state. Virtually all of these artifacts have lain underground or underwater since the Viking age, as discussed in the next chapter. What survives is often fragmentary: pieces of helmets, remnants of mail shirts, spears without shafts, and blades without tips or fittings.

Because historical bladesmithing techniques were used on the modern replica sax shown on the facing page, it is quite possible that the historical weapon in the same photograph looked something like the modern one when it was made more than one thousand years ago.

One way that the modern replicas fail to match the historical artifacts is in the level of detail of the decorations. Vikings prized decorations. Viking-age artifacts seem to be decorated on every available surface, even on the hidden surfaces of these items, and even on everyday, mundane items. This level of decoration is rarely applied to modern reproductions.

A detail of a writing tablet is shown on the facing page. Vikings wrote on wax-filled wood-

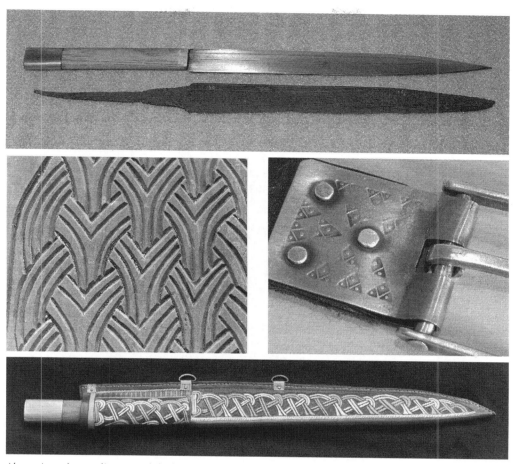

Above: A modern replica sax and the historical sax on which it was based are compared, showing what the historical sax might have looked like when new. The historical sax is in the collection of the Higgins Armory Museum. Middle: A modern replica of a Viking-age writing tablet (left) and belt buckle (right) illustrate the decorations typical on even the most mundane of Viking-age objects. Below: The replica sax sheath is based on a find from Trondheim in Norway and further illustrates the elaborate decorations favored by Vikings.

en writing tablets with an iron stylus. The back of the tablet is never seen when in use, but it is decorated with ornate carvings. Similarly, once the belt is fastened in place, the buckle plate isn't visible, yet the craftsman took the time to stamp decorations into its surface.

Prestige items, such as weapons, typically carried the level of decoration to an extreme, as on the reproduction sheath for a sax shown above. Few modern makers of Viking-age reproductions have the time, the skill, and the patience to recreate that level of decoration. Thus, few of the photos of modern reproductions used on these pages show the elaborate decorations that are typical of items crafted in the Viking age.

A modern replica of a Viking-age heathen idol stands by the road entering Haukadalur in west Iceland. Viking-age heathens were buried with grave goods, a practice that has preserved many aspects of Viking material culture that otherwise would have been lost, notably their weapons.

2

AVAILABLE SOURCES

Popular and fantasy sources would suggest that Viking weapons and their use are well understood today. To the contrary, Viking weapons and combat techniques are among the least well known of the historical European martial arts.

Our knowledge of Viking arms and their use comes from a small number of sources. The sources are simultaneously sparse and contradictory. Alone, none of these sources paints a clear picture of the arms or of the combat techniques. Taken together, our understanding, although speculative, becomes more clear.

Archaeological Finds

Most of our knowledge about the weapons of the Viking age comes from archaeological sources. That knowledge is limited relative to what is known about later arms and armor because, in comparison, little Viking-era armament survives. Unlike the later medieval and Renaissance periods when arms and armor were stored under cover and protected from the elements, virtually all of the Viking-age items survive only as excavated items—material dug up from underground or dredged up from underwater. Most of the artifacts are grave goods, but some may be ritual offerings, and others represent items lost or discarded during travel or in battle.

Most Viking people practiced the northern heathen religion, worshiping the gods and goddesses of the Norse myths and making offerings to idols that may have been similar to the modern reproduction shown on the facing page.

The burial practices of these heathen people included being interred with grave goods: items related to their work and social position when alive. Thus, prominent men and warriors were buried with their arms and armor. *Egils saga* says that Skalla-Grímr Kveld-Úlfsson, a farmer, blacksmith, and warrior, was buried at Digranes with his weapons, his horse, and his blacksmithing tools.

Whether intentionally or accidentally buried, it is this excavated material that we have available for study today. However, underground or underwater, these materials degrade. The wood and leather rot, and the iron rusts. So, it is only under unusual conditions that any Viking-age arms and armor have survived at all.

Although over one thousand Viking-age swords survive in various states of preservation, only a small handful of Viking-age helmets have survived. With so few items to study, it's difficult to determine if a particular specimen is normal or atypical for its historical period.

Combat Treatises

Our knowledge of Viking-age combat techniques is even more limited. The Vikings left

Left: Egils saga says that Skalla-Grímr Kveld-Úlfsson was buried with his weapons, his blacksmithing tools, and his horse. (*Illustration: Guðmundur Sigurðsson*) Right: Joachim Meyer's combat manual, published in 1570, is probably the most complete, the most important, and the most intelligible of the medieval European combat treatises. (*Higgins Armory Museum*)

nothing behind to teach us how they used their weapons.

The situation was very different later in the medieval era and in the Renaissance, when master fighters created training manuals that were used to teach combat techniques. Some of these manuals survive, such as the combat treatise written by the German master Joachim Meyer in 1570, and by studying them, one can gain an understanding of the fighting techniques used in those periods.

The manuals, however, are *not* "how-to" books. They are, rather, memory aids, allowing someone already possessing skill and knowledge in martial arts to recall the techniques taught by the master. The texts are obscure, capable of multiple interpretations and probably were made so intentionally to prevent unauthorized persons from benefitting from the knowledge contained in the book. Regardless, these treatises have opened the door to research, enabling modern scholars to re-create the forgotten martial arts of the European Middle Ages that have not been practiced for centuries.

Nothing like these treatises survives from the Viking era, so little can be said that is definitive about the use of Viking-age weapons.

One approach to re-creating Viking-era fighting techniques is to make reproduction weapons based on historical examples, and then to use those reproductions to try various combat techniques in an attempt to reinvent the historical techniques. It is highly unlikely that we can reconstruct the kind of effective fighting techniques that were refined over centuries and practiced by fighting men from childhood in the Viking age.

Another approach is to study the techniques taught in the later medieval fight manuals and adapt them to Viking-age weapons. Although Viking-age weapons and techniques differ considerably from those taught in later manuals, the later techniques did not spring up out of a vacuum. It's highly likely that the later techniques built upon prior practices. The later manuals attest to this sort of borrowing of techniques from earlier weapons. Because the historical manuals represent time-tested, martially effec-

The weapons taught in Meyer's combat manual differ from those used in the Viking age, and the combat techniques are likely to have been different as well. A reenactor dressed in 16th-century clothing and armed with a 16th-century weapon uses techniques from Meyer against a reenactor in 10th-century clothing with 10th-century weapons.

tive fighting systems, we chose to use them as our starting point.

However, when using the later manuals as sources, it is important to remember that they have a fundamental drawback: they teach weapons very different from those in use during the Viking age.

The photo on this page graphically illustrates those differences, showing a Viking armed with 10th-century sword and shield facing a combatant armed with a longsword and using techniques from Meyer's 16th-century combat manual. The weapons are different, and the techniques are likely to have been different as well.

For example, it appears that the Viking shield was used independently of the offensive weapon. The shield in the left hand can execute one trick while the sword in the right executes something completely different. In the simplest possible scenario, offense is in one hand and defense is in the other. That approach differs significantly from most of the material taught in the later combat treatises. In the German longsword treatises, the longsword is used simultaneously for offense and defense.

The earliest surviving European combat treatise is the *Royal Armouries MS I.33*, which dates from around the year 1320. The manual teaches techniques for sword and buckler, a small shield. Because this manual is closer in time to the Viking age and the weapons are closer in functionality to those of the Viking age than any of the other surviving manuals, one might think that the techniques would be closer to those used in the Viking age.

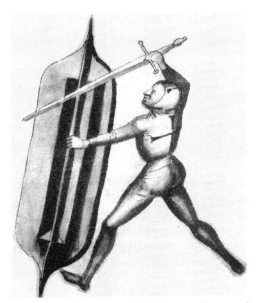

An illustration from Hans Talhoffer's combat manual of 1467 teaches a technique for longsword and dueling shield.

The opposite seems to be the case. For example, the *I.33* manuscript teaches that whenever the sword is forward, the buckler is at the sword hand to protect it. There appears to be no use of the buckler independent of the sword to block an incoming attack. As a result many of the techniques from *I.33* do not seem to apply well to Viking weapons, which likely use sword and shield more independently.

Hans Talhoffer's manual from 1467 teaches techniques for longsword and dueling shield, which are used independently. The longsword was longer than a Viking sword, and the dueling shield was considerably larger than a Viking shield. Yet, despite the significant differences between the weapons taught by Talhoffer and those used by Vikings, many of Talhoffer's techniques seem well suited for use with Viking weapons because in both cases sword and shield are used independently.

Another significant drawback to using the combat treatises as sources is that these western martial arts have no living tradition. They have not been practiced for centuries, and thus, there are no living masters who can pass on the techniques as originally practiced in the Middle Ages to a new generation of students. Although scholars can study the treatises and interpret the techniques, there is no guarantee that their techniques match those practiced by the masters who wrote the treatises.

THE SAGAS

Another source of information about fighting techniques is the literature from the Viking age and the period immediately following.

The Icelanders created and preserved most of the literature that survives from the northern lands in the Middle Ages. These texts survived the intervening centuries in the form of vellum manuscripts, virtually all of which were written in Iceland.

During the Viking age, Scandinavian culture was almost entirely oral. Although the runic alphabet was widely known, the Vikings didn't write down lengthy texts. Instead, important thoughts were remembered through poetry, which was transmitted orally.

Icelanders had a high reputation as poets throughout the northern lands. Many of their verses have survived, showing that they were indeed prolific poets in the Viking age.

With the conversion to Christianity in the 11th century, Iceland was introduced to a book-based culture. The Icelanders were quick to exploit the new means of preserving the story of their land and people.

In contrast with the rest of Europe, where vernacular literature took centuries to develop, the Icelanders were writing extensively in their native tongue within decades of their first works in Latin. In the year 1117, the Alþing (national assembly) called for Iceland's laws to be written down, a process that began the following winter. Around the year 1130, Ari enn fróði (the wise) Þorgilsson produced a history of Iceland, *Íslendingabók*. The other major text on the settlement of Iceland, *Landnámabók*, was composed at about the same time. By the beginning of the 13th century, Icelandic authors were producing a torrent of works in Icelandic.

Three general classes of medieval Icelandic literature are especially useful in studying the combat techniques of the Vikings.

The kings' sagas relate the life stories of the kings and royalty of Scandinavia. Notably, *Heimskringla* is a collection of sagas written by the Icelander Snorri Sturluson that tell the history of the kings of Norway, from their divine origins through to the late 12th century. Set primarily in Norway, where large-scale dynastic wars were more commonplace than in Iceland, they are useful sources in that they provide information about the techniques employed in mass battles.

The contemporary sagas, such as *Íslendinga saga*, were written about events taking place in Iceland during the 12th and 13th century. They were written by authors who had witnessed and participated in many of the historical battles they describe.

Most memorable of all are the medieval Icelanders' stories about their Viking-age ancestors, called *Íslendingasögur* (*Sagas of Icelanders*, also known as family sagas). The stories of the sagas take place in the 9th to 11th centuries, squarely in the Viking age. They were written during the 13th and 14th centuries and remain highly entertaining reading today.

The sagas feature farmers, chieftains, and slaves; husbands, wives, and rivals; friendships, hatreds, and conflicting loyalties; adventure, humor, and tragedy. Many of them follow families for generation after generation, beginning with their emigration from Norway. They are distinctive among medieval literatures in telling heroic tales not about heroes, but about typical Icelanders of the settlement period, offering compelling images of life in the Viking age.

The sagas must be used with great care as a historical source, however, given the centuries that separate the authors from their subjects, and given the changes that had taken place in Icelandic culture and society. Although the broad outlines of the stories may be based on actual events and historical characters, the details are obscured by time and were certainly manipulated to suit the authors' literary needs. Nonetheless, there is clearly a considerable body of genuine historical information embedded in these texts, and they remain one of the most important points of reference for understanding the Viking age.

One might think that the stories in these books would be especially useful as a source for fighting techniques. They were written by authors who had almost certainly witnessed combat, and who probably had personally participated in combat. In addition, they were written for an audience who, similarly, had probably either witnessed or participated in combat and who were familiar with fighting techniques. So, the combat situations described are probably realistic.

The stories, however, were written for entertainment, and a detailed description of combat technique is rarely necessary for advancing the plot. As a result, the sagas tend to say a lot about the participants in a fight and the ramifications of a fight, but very little about the techniques used.

In the rare instances where the sagas describe fighting techniques, are they describing earlier techniques from when the stories took place, or later techniques from when the stories were written down? Fortunately, we have some clues to help us decide.

A reenactor demonstrates techniques for sword and buckler taught in the Royal Armouries I.33 manuscript. The treatise seems to teach that when the sword is forward, the buckler is used to protect the sword hand.

The earliest combat treatise, the *Royal Armouries MS I.33* teaches techniques for sword and buckler, as I mentioned, which differ significantly from Viking sword and shield. The sword was slightly longer than a Viking-age sword, and the buckler was a small shield considerably smaller than a Viking-age shield. The I.33 treatise teaches practices that appear to have been well developed at the time the manuscript was created in the early part of the 14th century.

Although the text says little about the defensive uses of the buckler, the illustrations make clear that when the sword is forward, the buckler is placed next to the sword hand, between that hand and the opponent's sword, protecting the sword hand. Thus, during a fight, the combatant holds his buckler over his sword hand, and he rolls his buckler back and forth around his sword hand to maintain the protection to hand and forearm as the fight progresses. This technique is very different from that likely to have been used with a large Viking shield.

Were the Icelandic saga authors aware of these changes in weapons and fighting techniques that had occurred since the Viking age? Almost certainly yes. Perhaps the most compelling example comes from chapter 138 of *Íslendinga saga*, a contemporary saga. During the battle at Örlygsstaðir, which took place on August 21, 1238 in the north of Iceland, thousands of men met in a battle between competing *goðar* (chieftains) for supremacy. The author of the saga, Sturla Þórðarson, participated in the battle. During the height of the battle, Sturla says that Lauga-Snorri held his sword under the buckler, the way men do when they fence (*hafði sverðit undir buklaranum, sem þá er menn skylmast*).[3]

This is precisely the technique taught in the I.33 manuscript. The technique makes little sense when used with a large Viking shield but has clear merits when used with a buckler.

Sturla seems well aware that shields were distinguished from bucklers. Earlier in the battle at Örlygsstaðir, he says that Björn Leifsson held a shield over the fallen Sighvatr Sturluson, an act that would have provided negligible protection had the shield been a buckler.

These passages suggest that 13th-century Icelanders were aware of the new weapons and techniques that were being used in Europe and had adopted them for their own use. One passage from *Íslendinga saga* implies that skilled German fighters were present in Iceland, per-

3. Guðni Jónsson, ed. *Íslendinga saga*. (Reykjavík: Íslendingasagnaútgáfan, 1953) ch. 138 p. 347.

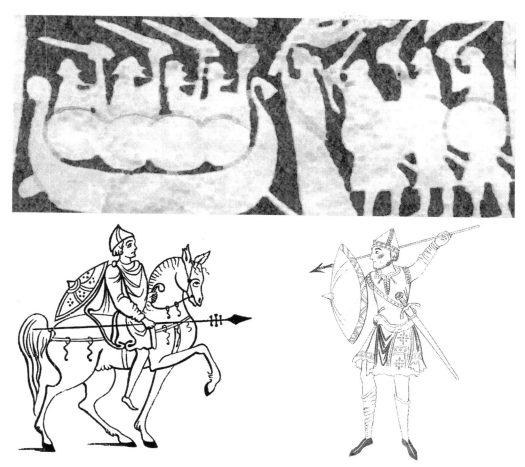

Above: A detail from the 10th-century picture stone at Lärbo in Gotland, Sweden, shows Viking warriors and their weapons. Below: Illustrations from 10th-century Anglo-Saxon manuscripts depict Saxon men-at-arms and their weapons.

haps to train men in these new combat techniques. In chapter 34, Sturla says that one of Snorri Sturluson's followers was a man named Herburt from Germany, more skillful than all other men in the use of the buckler.

If Sturla was aware of the differences in techniques between Viking times and contemporary times, it is quite possible that other saga authors were as well. Thus, there is some reason to believe that in describing Viking-age combat in the *Sagas of Icelanders*, the authors described weapons and techniques that were appropriate for the Viking age.

That does not imply that in every case the saga authors distinguished between weapons and techniques of the Viking age and those of their own times. Almost certainly, anachronisms crept in to their writing, and in many cases, the authors simply may not have been aware of the differences.

Regardless, the sagas can be valuable to help confirm speculations based on other sources. If, for instance, material from a later combat manual teaches the use of a weapon, and that same usage appears in a saga, it affirms our speculations based on other sources.

A detail from the Bayeux tapestry shows Norman arms and armor being loaded onto ships in preparation for the Norman invasion of England.

PICTORIAL SOURCES

An additional source of information comes from art: stone carvings, wood carvings, and tapestries from the Viking age. However, little pictorial art either of or by the Viking people survives.

What does survive tends to be representations of Norse mythology and heroic tales. Grave markers and memorial stones sometimes show warriors dressed for battle with their arms.

Some figurative art from other European societies during the Viking age has survived, such as the mounted Saxon warrior and the Saxon man-at-arms, shown in illustrations from 10th-century manuscripts on the previous page.

The Bayeux tapestry is another important pictorial source. The "tapestry" is actually a series of embroidered linen panels stitched together, and it depicts the events surrounding the Norman conquest of England in 1066. As such, it illustrates Normans and Saxons, rather than Vikings. Regardless, it is a valuable source of information concerning the weapons, equip-ment, and techniques of other northern European peoples in the Viking age.

FORENSICS

A final source of information comes from the forensic studies of Viking-age skeletal remains having battle injuries. This field is an increasingly valuable source. Forensics can confirm information from other sources about targets, injuries, and weapons use.

The 11th-century skull shown on the facing page has two disabling injuries (indicated by arrows), both made with a blade, probably a sword.

Some of the skeletal injuries show clearly the imperfections in the sword blade that created the injury. Striations visible in the bone across the cut are likely due to nicks and burrs on the blade that made the cut. These striations definitively mark the direction of the attack and show that the attack was a percussive cut, rather than a slice.

The sagas tell of combatants continuing to fight after multiple horrific disabling wounds. Such tales could easily be discounted as heroic exaggerations, but the historical skeletal remains confirm that at least some Viking warriors actually suffered the kinds of gruesome injuries described in the sagas. Further, the forensic evidence shows that some of these grievously wounded men survived, recovered, and lived to fight and suffer additional wounds later in their lives.

One source of forensic evidence that was discarded for this study comes from skeletal remains from the Battle of Visby, which took place in 1361 when Danish troops took the town of Visby, on the island of Gotland in Sweden. An extensive forensic study was conducted on the skeletal remains of some of the more than 2,000 casualties of the battle. However, by the 14th century, weapons and techniques had changed considerably from those used in the Viking age. Thus, I chose to set aside this information in favor of forensic studies of Viking-age skeletal remains.

LIMITATIONS TO THIS STUDY

Other sources of information that have not been used in this study are some of the fighting systems with a living tradition: styles that have been continually practiced since their inception. This category includes many Asian combat systems, some of which have significant European content due to colonial influences. Some of these systems use weapons similar to Viking weapons. I have not discarded these sources but rather have chosen to focus first on combat systems from places and periods more closely related to the Viking era, even though these systems have not been continually practiced as have some of the Asian systems.

In studying the combat techniques, I have focused on the use of Viking-age arms by small groups of men on dry land in single combat while on foot. That focus might at first seem overly restrictive. This form of combat, howev-

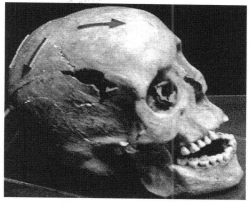

The skull of an 11th-century man shows two battle injuries. One probably caused extensive bleeding, and the other may have caused his death.

er, was more common than other forms, and thus more sources of information are available. In addition, the forms of combat excluded from this study tend to share many of the techniques and combat forms that were studied and are described in this text.

For example, Viking-age sea battles were fought on stationary ships, and so were more like land battles waged on floating islands. These battles had three stages. First, the ships were maneuvered into position, with the steersmen on board each ship trying to get the most favorable position, both relative to other ships, friend and foe, and relative to nearby land. They desired calm waters, in a protected fjord, or in the lee of an island, where marksmanship would not be spoiled by rocking decks. Next, a variety of projectiles were fired or thrown from one ship to another, including arrows, spears, and stones. During this time, the sails were furled, and in some cases the masts were unstepped. Last, ships grappled one another and were drawn together for hand-to-hand combat on the decks, using weapons and techniques similar to those used in land battles described in this text.

During the Viking age, most fights were between small groups of men. There were no regimented armies or professional soldiers, especially during the early part of the Viking age.

Large bands of Vikings are often described as armies, such as the Great Army that set up an encampment in Repton, England, in the winter of 873–874, an encampment that has received extensive archaeological study. However, these roving bands can scarcely be called *armies* in the modern sense of the word. The evidence suggests that though there were many men skilled at arms in the Viking era, few were trained, disciplined troops capable of waging an extended battle in formation under the command of a king or other leader.

The "army" of farmers at the Battle of Stiklarstaðir in Norway was so untrained and undisciplined as to be unable to advance in formation to the battle site yet was sufficiently competent with arms as to be able to kill the king, defeat his army, and send the remnants fleeing.

This lack of formal organization and discipline in Viking bands is reflected in the words of some Danish Vikings who had arrived in Frankish lands along the Loire. A Frankish representative arrived to inquire about the Vikings' intentions and asked to speak to the leader of the group. He was told, "We are all leaders here."

An example of some archaeological evidence that might suggest the presence of regular standing armies in Viking lands are the five fortresses found in Denmark and Sweden, the most notable being at Trelleborg in Sjælland. These fortresses are such massive undertakings and so similar in design that only a central authority such as a king could have planned and executed their construction. They were built at the end of the 10th century, during the reign of Haraldr Gormsson, also known as Harald Bluetooth. Did they serve as barracks for Haraldr's army? Probably not. Although some of the many houses inside the walls of the fortress were used as dwellings, many were workshops where domestic products were made. The skeletal remains of women and children are found in the burial grounds, suggesting that families lived within the fortress. Most telling is the fact that the buildings were never repaired, which suggests that they were used for only thirty years at most, then abandoned.

Currently, it is believed that the fortresses were royal administration centers, where taxes were collected, and where the symbols and trappings of a strong royal authority could be used to control the local population. Once Haraldr subjugated all of Denmark under his rule, he had no further need for the fortresses, and they were abandoned.

Taken together, the available evidence does not suggest that Vikings had trained, disciplined troops capable of fighting in formation under a commander's orders on the battlefield. In mass battles, men aligned themselves in shield walls or other formations and then advanced and engaged. Once the line had broken, the battle quickly degenerated into mêlées between small groups of men, using the weapons and techniques similar to those used in single combat and described in this text.

In the Viking lands, men fought on foot. There were no mounted troops or cavalry units. That didn't stop fighting men from making attacks either from horseback, or to a mounted opponent when the opportunity presented itself. Typically, men rode to where they were to fight, dismounted, and began the fight.

I tend to refer to the use of weapons by men because there are very few references to the use of weapons by women in the saga literature, as discussed in the previous chapter.

Gísli Súrsson fought to his death on Einhamar, the rock outcropping in Geirþjófsfjörður in west Iceland.

Last, I tend to emphasize the use of weapons in Iceland. Although the archaeological record is less rich than in other Viking lands, the literary records for weapon use in Iceland far exceed those of all the other Viking lands. The Icelandic sagas paint a lively picture of weapons use by ordinary people during the normal course of their everyday lives.

Despite the sparse and contradictory nature of available sources, some bold scholars have stepped into the breach and offered highly speculative interpretations of weapons use in the Viking age. In this text, I have chosen to present some of more intriguing of those speculative conclusions, even though they are poorly supported by the evidence, at present. Perhaps additional evidence will be found in the future to lend more weight to the speculations.

In the text, I have used many photographs of battle sites from the Icelandic sagas because they help to inform how men used their weapons. In some cases, the landscape has changed so much that it is no longer possible to visualize the conflict, such as the battle at Þingvellir described in chapter 145 of Brennu-

Njáls saga. The valley floor has subsided, and the river now floods more of the land than in saga times.

In other cases, the land looks nearly the same today as it did in the time of the sagas. One can see the attacks, the defenses, and the movements of men as the fight progressed, just as the saga author described them.

One such place is Geirþjófsfjörður in west Iceland, where Gísli Súrsson single-handedly battled against fifteen men. The landmarks are as described in the saga, and one can visualize how the battle moved from one rocky crag to another as Gísli tried to hold the high ground until Eyjólfr Þórðarson and his men overwhelmed Gísli on top of Einhamar.

Consideration of the available sources taken together yields a clearer picture of the shape of combat in the Viking age than has been available in the past. However, the conclusions are speculative. The techniques described here represent the author's opinion about what techniques may have been used in the Viking era, based on the limited historical material available.

This Viking shield, found in a near perfect state of preservation, is from the Gokstad ship burial in Vestfold, Norway, and dates from around the year 900. (© *Museum of Cultural History—University of Oslo, Norway*)

3

SHIELDS

In the Viking age, fighting men used large, round, wooden shields gripped in the center from behind an iron boss. However, shields represent one of several instances where the literary sources and archaeological sources do not agree on how Viking weapons were constructed.

The 10th-century Norwegian *Gulaþing* laws specify the construction of a shield. The shield should be made of wood with three iron bands and a handle fastened to the back side by iron nails. A later revision of the law says that the shield should be made of a double layer of boards (*tvibyrðr*), and the front should be painted red and white.

A few shields have survived from the Viking age, notably the shields from the Gokstad ship burial. The ship was equipped with 32 shields, several of which survive intact. They were made from a single layer of planks butted together, with no iron bands, and the fronts were painted black and yellow.

Typical Viking shields were 80 to 90 cm (32 to 36 in) in diameter. Some were larger, such as the Gokstad shields, which were 94 cm (37 in) across. Based on surviving remnants, some of the smaller shields appear to have been as small as 70 cm (28 in) in diameter.

All the surviving examples are made from solid butted planks, although literary evidence, such as the 10th-century Frankish poem

Waltharius and the *Gulaþing* laws, suggests that shields were made of laminated wood. No archaeological evidence supports this style of construction during the Viking era in Norse lands.

Surviving shields are made from spruce, fir, or pine. Again, literary evidence contradicts and suggests that shields were made of linden wood (*Tilia*, commonly known as basswood in North America). The word *lind* (linden) is used to mean *shield* in poems such as *Völuspá* (verse 50), and the term *lindiskjöldr* (linden shield) is used in some sagas. Linden certainly has advantages over other species of wood for shield use. It is lightweight and does not split as readily under impact as do other types of wood.

The Gokstad shields were approximately 7 mm (1/4 in) thick near the center and were chamfered so they were thinner at the edges. Most surviving shields are in the range between 6 mm (1/4 in) and 12 mm (1/2 in) thick, although shields thicker than 30 mm (1-1/8 in) have been found.

At the center of the shield was a domed iron boss, which protected the hand. Bosses were typically 15 cm (6 in) in diameter and had a thickness of 3 mm to 5mm (about 0.1 to 0.2 in, or between 6 and 12 gauge). The boss must be large enough to comfortably admit the hand and allow the shield to rotate freely around the

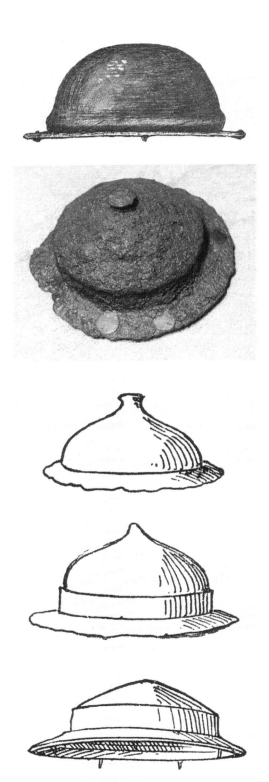

Left: Examples of Viking-era shield bosses. The top-most boss was found at Hemla in south Iceland. (*Illustration: Michéle Hayeur-Smith, Fornleifastofnun Íslands*) The boss shown second from the top dates from the Vendel era, which precedes the Viking age, but similar bosses, with long necks and a knob at the apex, were used in Viking times. The many nails that once held the boss to the shield are clearly visible. Above: The boss and handgrip were often fastened to the shield using clenched nails, as shown in this modern replica. Like the Gokstad shields, this replica has no iron reinforcements.

Viking shields were gripped from inside the iron boss. The arm did not pass through any straps, allowing the shield to be rotated freely from side to side during a fight.

hand as the combatant shifts his shield from side to side. Earlier bosses were hemispherical, whereas later bosses were more flattened. Some bosses had a cylindrical neck between the flange and the dome, such as the Vendel era boss shown opposite.

Flanges were usually round, although bosses with more elaborately shaped flanges, such as toothed flanges, have been found. Broad-headed iron nails passed through the flange and were either flattened, or clenched (bent over) on the reverse side of the shield to hold the boss in place.

The shield was gripped from the inside of the boss. The arm did not slip through any straps, and as a result, the shield could be rotated freely from side to side.

At least one passage from the sagas can be used to dispute this interpretation of the handgrip. In chapter 32 of *Bjarnar saga Hítdœlakappa*, the author says that Björn Hítdœlakappi held the shield with his forearm through the handgrip (*Björn helt á skildinum, svá at handleggr hans var í mundriðanum*).[4] Archaeological evidence, however, does not support the use of that kind of handgrip with round Viking shields, only with later kite-shaped shields, a form that probably

4. Sigurður Nordal and Guðni Jónsson, ed. *Bjarnar saga Hítdœlakappa* from *Íslenzk Fornrit III*. (Reykjavík: Hið Íslenzka Fornritafélag, 2001) ch. 32. p. 201

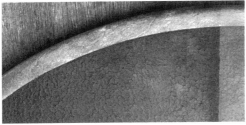

Above left: The handgrip was welded to the reverse side of the Vendel shield boss shown here and on the previous page. The boss is in a private collection. Above right: Iron reinforcing bars and an iron handgrip are attached to the reverse side of this replica Viking shield. Below left: Shields were probably rimmed with leather or rawhide, as shown on this modern replica shield.

did not see wide use in the Viking age, as discussed later in this chapter.

The interior of the Vendel era boss has a handgrip attached to the inside of the boss. Although some handgrips may have been as small as this Vendel grip, it's more likely that Viking-age handgrips extended nearly the full diameter of the shield.

Some shields used a simple wooden handgrip, whereas some may have used wood in combination with iron, fastened to the shield. Some of the surviving iron handgrips are decorated with silver or bronze. The handgrip was fastened across the planks, providing additional support to the assembled planks.

Although the *Gulaþing* laws required three iron reinforcing bars on the back of the shield, archaeological evidence is very slight. If they were used at all, these reinforcements would have added strength to the shield and served to hold the wood together.

The shield was probably rimmed with leather or rawhide that helped to keep the shield from splitting when hit on edge.

Although there is evidence that the wooden planks were glued edge-to-edge, a rawhide edging had the additional benefit of binding the shield very tightly together. The rawhide shrank after it was installed, forcing the planks together. The benefit of a rawhide edging should not be underestimated. Even after a shield had been punctured and split by a weapon, the edging held the pieces together so that the shield continued to offer some usable defense, as is demonstrated later in this chapter.

The Gokstad shields have a series of small holes all around the periphery of the shields. They are about 20 mm (3/4 in) in from the edge, spaced at 35-mm intervals (1-3/8 in). It is thought that a leather edging was held in place on these shields either with iron nails, or with stitching that passed through these holes.

Above left: A speculative reconstruction of an iron clamp holds the leather edging on this replica shield. Middle left: Iron fragments found at Baldursheimur in north Iceland have been interpreted as either fragments of an iron shield rim, or as iron reinforcements on the rear of the shield. (*Þjóðminjasafn Íslands*) Below left: This replica shield features a speculative interpretation of an iron rim. Right: A replica shield hangs at the back of a modern reenactor, slung over the shoulder using a leather sling.

Some historical shields have evidence of iron or bronze clamps around the edge, perhaps to hold the edging in place. Occasionally, these clamps were not uniformly distributed around the edge of the shield, suggesting that they were used to reinforce and protect a damaged edge.

Saga evidence suggests that iron-rimmed shields were used. When Bersi Véleifsson and Steinarr Önundarson dueled in chapter 12 of *Kormáks saga*, Bersi's sword stuck in the iron rim of Steinarr's shield.

In chapter 40, *Grettis saga* says that Snækollr carried an iron-rimmed shield to a duel against Grettir. Snækollr was a huge *berserkr*, a ferocious type of Viking warrior. Berserks are often stock characters in the sagas. They could enter a trance-like rage, assuming animal strength and ferocity. When a berserk enters a saga, you can count on his being killed a few chapters later. They frequently provide suitable opponents for the saga hero to prove himself.

There is negligible archaeological evidence, however, for iron-rimmed shields. The shield fragments found at Baldursheimur in north Iceland have been interpreted as either fragments of a shield rim, or as fragments of the reinforcement on the rear of the shield.

With so little of the original left to go on, either interpretation seems plausible. The shield boss was also found in the same grave site, along with the remnants of the nails that held the boss to the shield.

A leather sling, used to carry the shield over the shoulder was common. In chapter 14 of *Þorskfirðinga saga*, Þórir Oddsson went out to trim the manes of his horses. He worked with his shield hanging by his side. Bljúgr Helgason attacked unexpectedly, thrusting at Þórir with his spear. The spear glanced off the shield and entered the horse's belly, killing the animal.

There are many instances in the stories in which a fighter slung his shield over his back to wield his weapon with two hands, such as in chapter 53 of *Egils saga*. During a battle against Earl Hringr, Þórólfr Skalla-Grímsson threw his shield over his back and thrust with his spear using both hands, eventually thrusting it through the earl's chest and out his back.

The front of some shields may have been covered with leather. The leather facing made the shield significantly more resistant to the impact of weapons, although it also added some weight. The benefits of the leather facing are demonstrated graphically later in this chapter. Alternatively, shields may have been faced with linen, held in place with hide glue. The linen adds negligible weight, but the fibers greatly strengthen the wood, holding the structure together even if the wood splits.

Some surviving shields show evidence of paint (mineral pigments ground into an oil base such as linseed) on the wood surface, suggesting that they were not covered. Whether faced or not, shields were probably painted and decorated. The shields on the Gokstad ship were painted black and yellow. The sagas suggest that carrying a red shield signaled hostile intent. When a large group of shrieking natives arrived at the settlement of Hóp in Vínland, Þorfinnr

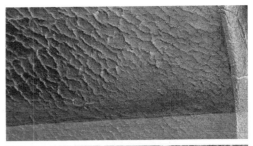

Above: Shields may have been covered in leather to strengthen the wood. The grain of the leather facing on this replica shield is clearly visible through the paint. Below: Alternately, shields may have been covered with linen, as was this replica shield. Linen adds much less weight to a shield than leather, while providing significant additional strength.

karlsefni and his men took up red shields and prepared for battle, as described in chapter 11 of *Eiríks saga rauða*.

Even if a shield were not decorated, it is highly likely that it would be sealed with oil so that it repelled and resisted water. A shield that soaked up water from rain or sea spray could easily double in weight, becoming so heavy and waterlogged as to be nearly useless.

The thin, unfaced reproduction shields shown in the photographs in this chapter weigh about 5 kg (11 lbs) when dry, whereas the thicker, leather-covered shields weigh more than 7 kg (15 lbs).

Left: Kite shields were used by other peoples in the Viking era, but probably not by Vikings. A reenactor carries a modern replica kite shield. Above: The Bayeux tapestry shows the use of kite shields in battle.

At the end of the Viking era, kite shields were used, as can be seen on the Bayeux Tapestry. When on horseback, the shape of the kite shield fit the space between the horse's neck and the rider's thigh, providing much better protection for the rider than a circular shield.

However, Vikings did their fighting on foot, where a circular shield provides better protection and better defensive options. It seems unlikely that kite shields would have seen wide use in Viking lands. One of the few kite shields found in Viking lands dates from late in the 11th century, after the end of the Viking age, and was found near Trondheim in Norway.

Evidence from skaldic poetry suggests round shields. Snorri Sturluson, writing well after the Viking age, says that in earlier times, shields were decorated on the border called the circle (*baugr*, which also has the meaning of *ring*).

Thus, Snorri says that in poetry, shields should be referred to as a *circle*, suggesting that shields were round. Snorri gives several examples of verse that use this reference. *Skáldskaparmál* verse 240 says, "A circle is most proper for a shield, and arrows for a bow" (*Baugr er á beru sœmstr / en á boga örvar*).[5]

Episodes in the sagas can be quoted to dispute this conclusion. One of these occurs in chapter 16 of *Flóamanna saga*. Þorgils Þórðarson fought a duel with Surtr járnhauss (Iron-skull). Þorgils sliced through the tip of Surtr's shield, as well as through Surtr's leg (*höggr Þorgils sporðinn af skildi Surts ok undan honum fótinn*).[6]

5. Snorri Sturluson. *Skaldskaparmál*. Anthony Faulkes. ed. (London: Viking Soceity for Northern Research. 1998) p. 70. verse 240.

6. Þórhallur Vilmundarson and Bjarni Vilhjálmsson. ed. *Flóamanna saga from Íslenzk Fornrit XIII*. (Reykjavík: Hið Íslenzka Fornritafélag, 1991) ch. 16. p. 261.

Left: A modern reenactor demonstrates a technique for sword and buckler, a small shield used after the end of the Viking age. Little evidence supports the use of bucklers in the Viking age. Right: Many Viking-age picture stones illustrate the large, round shield thought to be most commonly used by Vikings.

Round shields can scarcely be said to have "tips," suggesting that the shield in question was a kite shield. The significant word in the original Icelandic is *sporðr*, a word with multiple meanings. Some modern translations render this as *lower part of the shield*, but *tail of the shield* also fits.

Other kinds of shields are mentioned in the sagas, including *targa* (target) and *buklari* (buckler), although it is not clear from the stories how these differed from normal shields (*skjöldr*). In translation, the two words are usually rendered as *small shield*. Targets and bucklers are small shields known to have been used in later historical periods, although in the Renaissance, targets became larger.

Overwhelmingly, the archaeological and pictorial evidence, although sparse, supports only the use of large round shields by Viking warriors. Perhaps the saga language that suggests the use of kite shields or small shields is an anachronism, an error in which the saga author placed later shields from his own era into the earlier Viking era about which he was writing.

Pictorial evidence from other cultures in the Viking era, such as the Anglo-Saxons, suggests that shields may have been convex, having a pronounced dish shape. Again, archaeological evidence, though slight, does not support the use of convex shields in Viking lands.

THE Viking shield is a very effective defense. It blocks many lines of attack simultaneously. In a neutral, relaxed position, the shield protects from the neck to knees. The head and the lower legs are exposed and unprotected. Thus, the head and lower leg were likely targets. Although the shield can be moved rapidly to ward off blows coming in from a variety of directions, studies of skeletal remains show that many battle injuries occurred to the head and legs.

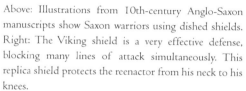

Above: Illustrations from 10th-century Anglo-Saxon manuscripts show Saxon warriors using dished shields. Right: The Viking shield is a very effective defense, blocking many lines of attack simultaneously. This replica shield protects the reenactor from his neck to his knees.

For example, the skull of an 11th-century fighting man who was about twenty years old at the time of his death has been recovered. The top of the skull was removed by a blow from a sword.

Leg injuries visible in the skeletal remains from Fishergate at York suggest deliberate attempts to sever the leg muscles, causing the combatant to fall without killing him.

Offensive weapons sometimes stuck fast in a shield after a blow. When that happened, a clever fighter could twist his shield either to break the weapon, or to break it loose from its owner's grip. In chapter 150 of *Brennu-Njáls saga*, Kári Sölmundarson caught a spear thrust with his shield, then snapped the spear by wrenching his shield.

The sagas suggest that a shield might have been used with two hands to defend against a particularly powerful attack. In chapter 55 of *Laxdæla saga*, Bolli Þorleiksson saw Helgi Harðbeinsson prepare for a thrust with his spear. Bolli dropped his sword to hold the shield with both hands. This trick did not stop Helgi's spear from penetrating the shield and wounding Bolli.

In chapter 24 of *Grettis saga*, Gunnarr held his shield with two hands against an attack by Grettir Ásmundarson. The trick didn't work in this case, either. Grettir hacked with his sax (short sword) between Gunnarr's body and the shield, cutting off both of Gunnarr's hands.

Occasionally, men dropped their shields in battle if they temporarily needed a free hand for some other purpose. In chapter 150 of *Brennu-Njáls saga*, Grani Gunnarsson shot a spear at Kári Sölmundarson. While the spear was in flight, Kári jammed his shield into the ground so hard that the shield stood up by itself. With his left hand, Kári grabbed the spear out of the air and shot it back at Grani, and then he snatched his shield back up, all while holding his sword in his

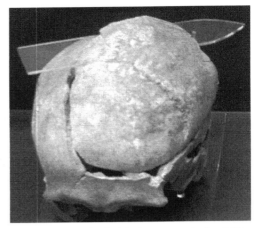

Many Viking-age battle injuries were to the head. The terminus of the sword blow that nearly removed the top of this 11th-century fighting man's skull is indicated by the clear blade.

other hand. The spear found its mark, and Grani was seriously wounded.

Many people think of a shield as a wall to hide behind. Although shields can be used passively in that manner, a more aggressive posture and use are advantageous.

In single combat, the shield was probably held at an angle to the body, either to the outside (to the left side for a right-handed man) or to the inside (to the right side). This stance puts the combatant in an aggressive position with good defensive options.

The aggressive posture moves the line of defense well away from the body. Attacks can be parried or deflected or broken up well before they reach the body. The angle prevents the shield from being driven straight into the combatant's body, which might pin his arms and limit his options. The angle also allows incoming blows to be deflected, rather than being caught straight on. Deflecting the blow, rather

In single combat, the shield was held at an angle to the body, nearly parallel with the line of engagement, the imaginary line that connects the two combatants. This stance puts the combatants in an aggressive position with good defensive options.

than stopping it, puts less stress on the shield, and on the combatant's arm, reducing the likelihood that either will break. Egill Skalla-Grímsson used this technique against Berg-Önundr Þorgeirsson in chapter 57 of *Egils saga*. Egill placed his shield at an angle so that the spear (*kesja*) thrown by Önundr was deflected by the shield and glanced off.

One example of an aggressive defensive use of the shield is binding the opponent's weapons, allowing new lines of attack to be opened. By sweeping his shield from outside to inside across his front, a combatant can capture and trap his opponent's weapons with his shield, leaving the opponent open to an attack from any one of many directions. This kind of *shield bind* can also be used to apply pressure to the opponent's body, allowing a combatant to control the movements of his opponent.

A consequence of this kind of shield use is that the shield rarely contacts a weapon. Instead, the shield is used against body parts. It is often the case that the opponent's weapon is neutralized not by controlling his weapon with the shield, but rather, by controlling his body with the shield.

That is not to say that the flat of the shield was never used for parrying a weapon in the Viking age. Surely, a warrior would parry with whatever was available in the heat of battle. Kári Sölmundarson had just finished cutting a man in two in the battle at Skaptártunga when Lambi Sigurðarson cut at Kári with his sword, as told in chapter 150 of *Brennu-Njáls saga*. Kári parried the attack with the flat of his shield. That the saga author found this notable enough to mention suggests that perhaps this usage of the shield was less common. The author also

Test cuts were made against an unfaced replica Viking shield using a replica Viking axe. Top: The shield was fixed to a wooden stand that simulated a human grip on the shield. The cut was made without a windup, as one might do in a combat situation. Middle right: The axe penetrated the shield easily. Below right: Had a hand been holding the shield, it would have been partially severed. Middle left: The first cut split one of the planks of the shield from end to end. The rawhide edging held the shield together. Below left: The second cut destroyed the shield, breaking the handgrip and bursting the edging, allowing the shield to fall apart.

commented that Lambi's sword did not "bite" the shield, again, suggesting that perhaps a different outcome was expected. There are certainly many examples in the sagas in which weapons split a shield. Regardless, Kári's parry with the flat of his shield was successful, and he subsequently thrust though Lambi's chest, killing him.

The futility of hiding behind a shield as if it were a wall is graphically illustrated in the series of photographs opposite. Test cuts were made, using a replica Viking axe against a replica Viking shield. The shield was constructed in accordance with available archaeological evidence, using wooden planks butted together.

The shield was 84 cm (33 in) in diameter and was 13 mm (1/2 in) thick. Planks of Quaking Aspen (*Populus tremuloides*) were used, a hardwood having similar properties to basswood (*Tilia*, also known as linden outside of North America). The boss was attached to the front by clinched forged nails, and the handgrip was similarly attached to the back.

A rawhide edging was attached to the rim by tacks. No iron reinforcements were used on the back, and no facing was used on the front. The shield was affixed to a wooden stand that simulated a human grip on the shield.

A cut was made from a guard (a starting position) without a windup, as one might do in a combat situation. The axe penetrated the shield easily.

The joins between the planks held firm, but the axe split one of the planks from end to end. The fragments were held in place by the rawhide edging.

If a hand had been holding the shield when the blow struck, the axe would have partially severed the hand.

With the second blow, the shield was destroyed. Again, the plank was split from end to end, and this time, the rawhide edging failed.

The handgrip broke in several places, and the shield fell apart.

This outcome is what we would expect, based on stories from the sagas. For example, in chapter 145 of *Brennu-Njáls saga*, Þorgeirr swung his axe at Þorvaldr, who caught the blow on his shield. The axe split the entire width of the shield, and the horn, the pointed tip of the axehead, penetrated Þorvaldr's chest, killing him.

The same test cuts were made on an identical shield that was faced with leather. 1 mm (2 oz) leather was glued to the front surface of the wooden planks.

The first blow penetrated the shield but did not split the planks. There was no damage to the shield, other than the penetration, and the shield remained an effective defense.

Even after four solid blows, the shield was still intact, without any splits. It remained a solid, usable defense, demonstrating the benefit of a leather facing on shield.

It wasn't until the sixth blow that the shield failed, due to the shattering of the handgrip. This failure suggests that a solid iron reinforcement would be beneficial for extending the utility of the shield faced with leather.

These kinds of test cuts only invite more questions. Would a person be able to maintain a grip on the shield under the impact of a blow like this? Would bones break? What would be an appropriate follow-up attack? We hope that further research and experiments will answer some of these questions.

In addition to its obvious defensive uses, the shield can also be used offensively. The edge of the shield can be used for punching, turning it into a very effective set of "brass knuckles."

If a combatant does not take care to control his opponent's shield, he may quickly find his teeth have been knocked out, or worse. In chapter 32 of *Bjarnar saga Hítdælakappa*, Björn

Top: The same test was performed against a replica Viking shield faced with leather. Bottom: The first blow penetrated the shield but did not split the planks. Facing Page: After four blows, the faced shield remained a solid, usable defense. Not until the sixth blow did the shield begin to break apart.

Hítdœlakappi drove the remnants of his shield into his opponent's head to kill him.

Any time an opponent is inattentive, it is possible to use the shield in this aggressive manner. If a combatant can bring his shield inside his opponent's shield, as the combatant on the right has done in the photograph shown on the next page, an attack with the edge of the shield can be made to the head, or upper body, such as the armpit. Although not lethal, it distracts the opponent, causes his shield to become useless, and opens new lines of attack.

Striking with the shield is a technique taught in *Royal Armouries MS I.33* and other early combat treatises. These kinds of aggressive use of the shield are discussed in greater detail later, in the chapter on sword and shield technique.

Other kinds of attacks with the shield are described in the sagas. The battle on the ice on the Markarfljót is described in chapter 92 of *Brennu-Njáls saga*. Þráinn Sigfússon and his men, while traveling across the frozen Markarfljót River saw an imminent ambush from Njáll's

sons, who were lying in wait on Rauðuskríðr, the hill on the far side of the river.

Skarpheðinn Njálsson fell behind to tie a broken shoe lace. When he arrived at the edge of the river, he saw an opportunity. Þráinn and his men were standing on a frozen ice bridge in the middle of the river. Skarpheðinn leapt onto the ice and slid across the frozen surface toward Þráinn, as fast as a bird flies. He placed his axe in Þráinn's skull and continued gliding across the ice. Tjörvi flung his shield at Skarpheðinn's feet, hoping to trip him, but the trick didn't work. Skarpheðinn jumped over the shield and reached the other side of the ice without losing his balance.

The stories also describe instances where the shield was used completely passively. Shields were thrown on fallen combatants during a battle to protect them from further injury. In chapter 150 of *Brennu-Njáls saga*, Kári Sölmundarson threw a spear at Grani Gunnarsson, which pierced his thigh and pinned him to the ground. Grani's companions freed the spear, and to pro-

Above: A Viking shield also has many offensive uses. The edge can be used for punching, turning the shield into an effective set of "brass knuckles." The combatant on the right is about to knock out his opponent's teeth with the edge of his shield. Left: Combatants sometimes held a second weapon behind their shield, ready for instant use in a fight.

tect Grani from further injury, they laid him in a hollow in the ground and covered him with shields.

A swimmer under attack from projectiles thrown from the shore might cover his back with his shield to protect himself while swimming. In chapter 26 of *Bjarnar saga Hítdœlakappa*, Björn Hítdœlakappi did just that while swimming across the Hítará to escape an ambush by þórðr Kolbeinsson and his men.

The stories suggest that slaves were used as human shields. In chapter 23 of *Víga-Glúms saga*, Glúmr Eyjólfsson fell in battle. His two slaves threw themselves on his fallen body to shield him. The slaves were both killed, but Glúmr survived.

Shields were used as barriers, to surround and subdue opponents, as described in chapter 89 of *Brennu-Njáls saga*. While fighting against Earl Hákon and his men, the sons of Njáll were encircled by the earl's son Sveinn and his men, who penned them in with their shields. The earl ordered the captured men killed at once, but Sveinn demurred, pointing out that it was night,

Top: Skarpheðinn and his brothers waited in ambush for Þráinn at Rauðuskríðr, the hill on the opposite shore of the Markarfljót river in south Iceland. When they attacked, Skarpheðinn slid over the frozen river and drove his axe into Þráinn. Tjörvi tried to stop Skarpheðinn by flinging his shield at his feet, but Skarpheðinn merely jumped over it. Bottom: Björn swam across the Hítará river in west Iceland at this spot to escape an ambush. Björn threw his shield on his back to protect himself from spears that were thrown at him from the shore.

when men should not be killed. The captives were bound, but later in the night, they were able to cut their bonds and escape.

During a weapons practice outdoors, I discovered what should be obvious: a shield makes an excellent sail. A gusty wind makes controlling the shield very much more difficult.

The stories say that a fighter might hold a second weapon at the ready in his shield hand, while fighting with his primary weapon in the other hand. In chapter 12 of *Fóstbrœðra saga*, Þorgeirr Hávarsson held a shield and an axe in his left hand while he fought with a spear in his

right hand. Later in the fight, he threw down his spear and took up the axe in his right hand, using it to cut through Snorri Hœkilsson's spear shaft, and then through Snorri's head.

The apparent size of the shield can often be extended. For example, a combatant can use his axe haft or his spear shaft to augment his shield in defense, blocking more lines of attack, and making the effective defense larger. Backing up the shield with a haft makes the defense stronger as well, because it becomes a two-handed defense.

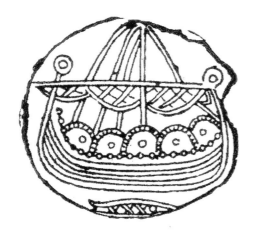

A 9th-century coin from Hedeby depicts a Viking ship with shields on display.

THE use of shields was nearly universal in Viking combat. Someone without a shield would be, quite literally, defenseless and would likely be cut down very quickly. So, most every fighting man would have had a shield.

The stories say that occasionally, some men chose not to carry a shield, notably when they carried a two-handed weapon, or a different weapon in each hand. Gunnarr Hámundarson carried his *atgeirr* (halberd) in one hand and a sword in the other at the battle at Eystri-Rangá described in chapter 63 of *Brennu-Njáls saga*. Thinking him defenseless, Þorgeirr Starkaðarson urged his brothers Börkr and Þorkell to charge at Gunnarr together. "He has no shield, and we'll have his life in our hands." Gunnarr had other ideas, and he knocked Börkr's sword out of his hand with his atgeirr while slicing off Þorkell's head with his sword.

Þormóðr Bersason prepared for a battle, as told in chapter 24 of *Fóstbræðra saga*. He carried a sword and an axe, but no shield. Seeing that he had no shield, King Óláfr inn helgi (the holy) asked why he was not dressed for battle like other men. Did he think the opponents they were about to face didn't know how to fight? Þormóðr replied that his axe would serve as his shield and mail shirt.

The later combat manuals suggest that Þormóðr was right. A long-hafted weapon has many defensive uses, described in more detail in the chapter on axes.

Because the shield could and did break in combat, people expecting to be in a protracted fight such as a duel might have several shields on hand. The sagas are filled with examples in which shields split or punctured under the force of incoming spears, axes, or swords. While fighting Gunnarr Þórisson in chapter 43 of *Grettis saga*, Atli Ásmundarson delivered a blow with his sword that sliced through Gunnarr's shield and part of Gunnarr's knee. Atli's next blow killed Gunnarr.

Shields were treated differently than other weapons, perhaps because they were so disposable. Shields apparently were not named, in the way that swords, mail, and other weapons often were.

SHIELDS had uses outside of combat. Elaborately decorated shields were given as gifts. In chapter 78 of *Egils saga*, Earl Hákon gave the poet Einarr Helgason a shield that was carved with scenes from legends, overlaid with gold, and set with jewels. Later in the saga, Einarr left the shield as a gift for Egill Skalla-Grímsson, hanging it on the wall above his bed.

Shields were used as decorations inside the longhouse. In chapter 11 of *Egils saga*, Þórólfr Kveld-Úlfsson held a great feast for the king. So many people were invited that Þórólfr had to install benches in a large barn so that there would be places for all the guests. Shields were hung on the walls for decorations.

Shields were used as stretchers, to carry away men wounded in combat. In chapter 24 of

The Sae Hrafn, a replica Viking ship operated by the Longship Company Ltd., sails out on the Chesapeake Bay in Vinland with shields displayed. (*Photo: Leonard Leshuk, Longship Company Ltd.*)

Ljósvetninga saga, Koðrán Guðmundarson tried to stop a fight by separating the combatants. When he stepped into the fray, he was struck on the head with an axe. Koðrán was carried away on a shield. His wounds were bound, but he died from his injuries in the night.

On board ship, shields were arrayed along the gunwales, shown in picture stones and coins from the Viking age. A shield rack along the gunwales provided a place to tie the handgrip of the shield to the ship.

The shields would have provided the crew with some additional protection from wind and waves, as well as from projectiles fired during battle. Several sources, however, suggest that shields were not routinely displayed while underway. Modern sailors of replica ships say they are very impractical. More likely, the shields were deployed only for battle, or to make the ship look especially fine and imposing when approaching land. *Landnámabók* tells of

Hella-Björn Herfinnsson who sailed into Bjarnarfjörður in west Iceland with his ship lined with shields. Afterwards, he was called *Skjalda-Björn* (Shield-Björn).

There are some students of Viking-age fighting styles who say that a shield was the only defense needed, and that proper use of a shield makes other defenses, such as helmet and mail, unnecessary. Others would disagree, saying that even with a shield, the other defenses are necessary. We don't know enough about fighting techniques to resolve this question. However, because helmet and mail were expensive, due to the cost and limited availability of iron, there were probably many combatants using only a shield for defense in the Viking age.

This 10th-century helmet found at Gjermundbu in Norway, although in fragments, is the best preserved Viking-age helmet found to date. (*Photo: Ove Holst, © Museum of Cultural History—University of Oslo, Norway*)

4

HELMETS

DURING the Viking age, helmets were typically fairly simple, consisting of a bowl with a prominent nose guard. One thing to note: Viking helmets had no horns. There is no evidence that Viking-era helmets ever had horns. Horn-like protrusions were used on helmets in other cultures and in other eras, but not in Viking lands and Viking times.

Before and after the Viking era, helmet bowls were made from a single piece of iron, hammered into shape. However, during the Viking era, helmets typically were made from several pieces of iron riveted together, called a *spangenhelm* style of helm.

It is easier to make a helmet this way, requiring less labor, which may be why it was used.

The spangenhelm used a single iron band that circled the head around the brow. Typically, two more iron bands crossing at the top of the head were riveted to the brow band. The four resulting openings were filled with riveted iron plates to create the bowl.

In some cases, hardened leather, rather than iron, may have been used to fill the four openings to reduce cost. The leather provided some limited protection at a fraction of the cost of iron.

The nose guard was riveted to the brow. At first glance, the nose guard looks awkward and nearly useless, but I can attest to its usefulness;

it has prevented my nose from being broken at least once.

Saga sources, however, suggest the nose guard could be cut away. In chapter 227 of *Óláfs saga helga*, King Óláfr cut across the head of Þorgeirr, slicing his nose guard in two, and his face as well.

It is not clear what was used inside the helmet. Something is needed to lift the helmet up off the head and to spread out and absorb the force of a blow. If the iron of the helmet were to rest directly on the head, a blow to the helmet would be transmitted directly to the skull, providing only limited protection. Some surviving helmet fragments have rivet holes that suggest that some sort of leather suspension was used. In addition, it is likely that a cap made from an absorbent material such as sheepskin was used, not only to absorb the blow, but also to absorb sweat, to help prevent the helmet from rusting from the inside.

The later combat manuals teach the importance of the head as a target, such as Talhoffer's manual from 1467. Illustrations in the book show many examples of attacks to the head.

Although the helmet provides some protection against a blow to the head, the stories suggest that a powerful blow could split the helmet and the skull inside.

In chapter 27 of *Egils saga*, Kveld-Úlfr Bjálfason, in a wild battle frenzy while onboard

Top left: A replica Norman helmet is formed from a single piece of iron. Top right: A replica Viking helmet is made in the spangenhelm style using pieces of iron riveted together. Bottom left: The iron plates of the replica spangenhelm are riveted to the iron bands. Bottom right: In some cases, hardened leather plates, rather than iron, were used to reduce cost, as shown on this modern replica helmet.

a ship, swung his *bryntröll* (mail troll, an unknown weapon that probably had an axe-like head) at Hallvarðr harðfari (hard-traveler). The weapon passed through Hallvarðr's helmet and skull, sinking up to the haft. Kveld-Úlfr pulled the weapon back with such force that Hallvarðr was lifted up by his head into the air and tossed overboard.

Above: Medieval combat manuals, such as Talhoffer's treatise from 1467, teach the effectiveness of an attack to the head. Left: This warrior, illustrated on the Bayeux tapestry, seems to have a chinstrap on his helmet to keep his helmet in place during combat.

Even a sword could penetrate a helmet when wielded by a powerful combatant. In chapter 9 of *Gunnars saga Keldugnúpsfífls*, Gunnar Keldugnúpsfífl (fool from Keldugnúpr) cut at Örn's head with his sword, splitting the helmet and Örn's skull all the way through.

In at least some cases, a combatant apparently expected his sword to slice through a helmet. In chapter 32 of *Finnboga saga ramma*, Jökull Ingimundarson struck at Þorgrímr's helmet with his sword. The saga author says that the sword cut no deeper than if it had been made of wood, which surprised Jökull greatly because he apparently expected his sword to penetrate the helmet.

Some form of chin fastening is required to keep the helmet in place during vigorous activity. There is little evidence, however, for chin straps. There is no convincing archaeological evidence and little pictorial evidence, although a rider depicted on the Bayeux tapestry might arguably have a chin strap.

On the other hand, helmets before and after the Viking age routinely used chin straps. From *Grágás*, the medieval Icelandic lawbook, we know that hats with chin straps were worn during the Viking age because there were laws regarding them. If a man pulled a hat with a chin strap backwards off another man, the act was considered throttling. The penalty was outlawry, and the victim had the right to kill in retaliation.

The most convincing evidence for me, however, is that without a chin strap, a reproduction helmet is quite useless in a fight; it simply falls off. Some reproduction helmets use a simple, thin leather thong that ties under the chin. Speaking as someone with a full beard, I don't find that approach viable because the leather thong constantly tugs at my beard. Most Viking-age warriors probably felt the same way. Virtually every man in the Viking age had a beard. The limited pictorial evidence available shows men with facial hair. Men who could not grow a beard were mocked, such as Njáll Þorgeirsson in chapter 44 of *Brennu-Njáls saga*. When Hallgerðr Höskuldsdóttir learned from some gossips that Njáll's men were fertilizing his farm fields by spreading manure, she said that instead they should spread manure on his face to fertilize there, so he could be like other men. The reproduction helmets shown in the photos, therefore, have wider chin straps. When properly adjusted, they hold the helmet securely without pulling on my beard all the time.

Other styles of Viking-age helmets have been found. The well-known 10th-century helmet found at Gjermundbu in Norway, shown facing the title page, has a spectacle-like covering for the face. The spectacle style is frightening for someone on the outside looking in, and for someone on the inside looking out. From the outside, it presents a frightening visage to the opponent because the face is covered and made

anonymous. It's even scarier from the inside because the spectacles catch incoming spear tips and sword points and guide them right into the wearer's eyes. They're very dangerous in simulated combat and would be in real combat, too, I imagine.

However, the original helmet has battle damage (a sword blow and an arrow puncture) to one of the plates, suggesting it was used in earnest combat. Perhaps my modern preconceptions about the danger of the spectacles are in error.

Some helmets from the period had mail curtains or solid plates on the neck and cheek to provide additional protection. These defenses provide significant protection against cuts to vulnerable parts of the head and neck. Other forms of solid cheek and neck protection may have been used as well.

A surviving helmet from the Vendel age, which predates the Viking era, has a mail curtain that completely encloses the face and neck, similar to the reproduction helmet on the facing page. It is possible that early in the Viking age, helmets of this type were still in use. Later, in the medieval period, this kind of mail curtain was known as an *aventail*.

The additional helmet defenses might not have been helpful in every case. Chapter 40 of *Grettis saga* tells of Grettir Ásmundarson's fight with Snækollr berserkr, who wore a helmet with the cheek guards undone. Grettir walked up to Snækollr, who was sitting on his horse, and immediately kicked the bottom of Snækollr's shield up into his mouth, which ripped open his face. Grettir grabbed Snækollr's helmet with his left hand and pulled him from his horse while cutting off Snækollr's head with the sax in his right hand. Although the saga author doesn't specify where Grettir grabbed the helmet, those loose, dangling cheek guards would have made a convenient handle.

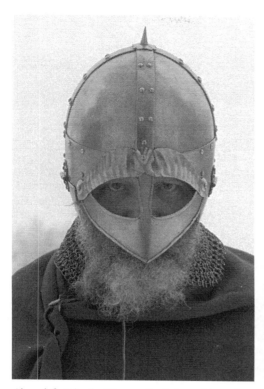

Above left: Like the Gjermundbu helmet, this modern replica has a spectacle-like covering for the face. Above right: The same replica helmet also has mail and solid plates which further protect the neck and head. Right: Before the Viking age, some helmets had a mail curtain that protected the entire face and neck, similar to the replica Vendel-era helmet shown here.

Helmets were probably quite comfortable for all-day wear. It is difficult to get an estimate of the weight of helmets because the only helmet that survives more-or-less intact, the Gjermundbu helmet, is missing portions. The portions that have survived are considerably eroded and are thinner than when the helmet was new. The helmet is slightly oval shaped, and its major diameter is 23 cm (about 9 in).

Modern helmet reproductions weigh about 2 kg (4 lbs), although some of the larger helmets

Before þráinn could put on his helmet, Skarpheðinn slid across the ice and drove an axe through þráinn's unprotected skull. (*Otto Bache, Skarphéðinn draeber Thráinn, 1862, National Gallery of Iceland*)

(with mail and additional protection) may have weighed more than 4 kg (10 lbs). They don't interfere with seeing, hearing, breathing, eating, or drinking. In the Viking era, fighting men probably wore their helmets all day.

The classic example from the sagas of a fighter killed before he could put on his helmet occurs in chapter 92 of *Brennu-Njáls saga*. Njáll's sons ambushed þráinn Sigfússon and his men as they crossed the frozen Markarfljót. Inexplicably, as the ambushers approached, þráinn took off his helmet and cloak. Before he could put his helmet back on, Skarpheðinn Njálsson seized the initiative and slid across the ice to drive an axe though þráinn's skull.

The stories suggest that helmets were marked in some manner before a large battle so combatants on each side could identify one another. In chapter 142 of *Brennu-Njáls saga*, the two sides made ready for the battle at the Alþing, arming themselves and putting marks (*herkuml*) on their helmets. It is not known what the nature of the markings might have been.

Before the battle at Stiklarstaðir, King Óláfr inn helgi told his men to put marks on their helmets and shields, as described in chapter 205 of *Óláfs saga helga*. "Draw the holy cross on them with chalk," the king commanded.

Because of the cost of the iron they contained, helmets were expensive and thus not common. Anyone who could afford one would certainly want one, but not too many people could afford one. Helmets were prized and carefully preserved, repaired as needed, and passed from generation to generation. Some may well have been used for centuries before the iron became too thin and weak to provide any real protection, at which time the remaining iron was used for other purposes. Perhaps it is for this reason that helmets are rarely found in graves.

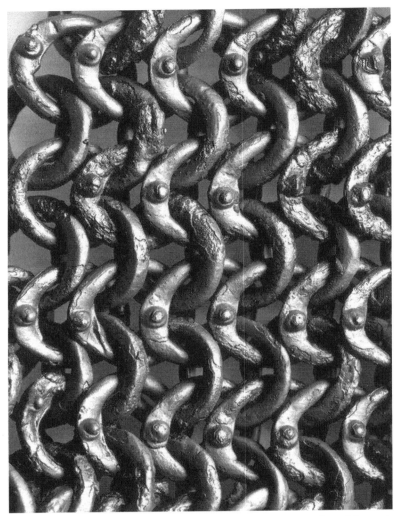

Although in fragments, the 10th-century mail shirt found at Gjermundbu in Norway is the best preserved Viking-age mail found to date. The photo shows a detail of the shirt. (*Photo: Vegard Vike*)

5

MAIL

MAIL is a protective iron fabric made up of thousands of interlocking iron rings. In the Viking era, mail was always made using a 4-in-1 pattern. Using this pattern, each ring passes through its four nearest neighbors.

During the Viking age, mail usually was worn in the form of a mail shirt (*brynja*). The details of the shape and size of mail shirts are not well known. Little mail survives from the Viking era. Underground or underwater, the thin iron rings corrode very quickly. Most surviving mail from the period is little more than a rusty pile of scrap.

The 10th-century mail shirt found at Gjermundbu in Norway is the only surviving Viking-age mail shirt that is substantially complete. It was in many pieces when found, and numerous sections were corroded into a solid mass. Some of the rings survive only as hollow corroded shells. The garment is so poorly preserved that it is not possible to reconstruct its form. As a result, any discussion of typical mail shirt lengths is speculative. Pictorial evidence suggests that mail shirts were T-shaped with short sleeves—half to three-quarters length—and were thigh length. Anything longer would make it difficult to ride a horse.

Saga sources suggest that some exceptional mail shirts were longer. King Haraldr harðráði had a mail shirt that reached down below his knees, which he called Emma, as told in chapter 91 of *Haralds saga Sigurðarsonar*.

The reproduction mail shirt shown on page 59 weighs about 12 kg (26 lbs). A lot of the weight is taken up on the hips by the belt, in much the same way as a modern backpack, so the weight is not particularly burdensome.

Regardless, the stories say that sometimes raiders left their mail shirts onboard ship when they went raiding, so they wouldn't be weighted down. On the day of the battle at Stamford Bridge, the weather was fine, with hot sunshine, as told in chapter 87 of *Haralds saga Sigurðarsonar*. The Norwegians left their mail shirts behind, onboard ship. *Ljósvetninga saga* adds in chapter 31 that only the Icelander named Brandr Gunnsteinsson was wearing a mail shirt. He offered it to King Haraldr, but the king declined. "For certain, you are an honorable man, but keep the mail shirt for yourself." Both men died in the battle.

The 12 kg of iron in a mail shirt represented a treasure in the Viking age. Few people could have afforded that much iron. Thus, mail shirts must have been very rare. Anyone who could have afforded one would certainly have wanted one, but probably few people could afford one.

Someone who couldn't afford a mail shirt might have used smaller pieces of mail to protect the parts of the body more susceptible to

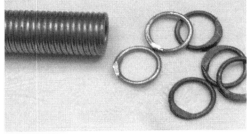

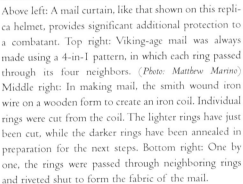

Above left: A mail curtain, like that shown on this replica helmet, provides significant additional protection to a combatant. Top right: Viking-age mail was always made using a 4-in-1 pattern, in which each ring passed through its four neighbors. (*Photo: Matthew Marino*) Middle right: In making mail, the smith wound iron wire on a wooden form to create an iron coil. Individual rings were cut from the coil. The lighter rings have just been cut, while the darker rings have been annealed in preparation for the next steps. Bottom right: One by one, the rings were passed through neighboring rings and riveted shut to form the fabric of the mail.

attack, such as a mail curtain attached to a helmet to protect the most vulnerable part of the neck from cuts. It provides significant protection while using only a fraction of the iron of a full mail shirt.

To make mail, a smith started with an iron bar, which he drew into iron wire by drawing it repeatedly through smaller and smaller openings in an iron drawplate, until the wire diameter had been sufficiently reduced for the intended purpose.

The wire was wound around a wooden form to create a coil of iron wire. The coil was split down its length to create a number of open iron rings. One by one, each ring was passed through neighboring rings to form the fabric of the shirt, then closed and sealed shut with a rivet. This process was repeated again and again, thousands and thousands of times, to make up the fabric of the shirt.

The reproduction mail shirt shown opposite is made from about 30,000 rings, each riveted shut. Fabricating mail in the Viking age must have been extremely labor intensive.

Viking-age mail often took the form of a T-shaped shirt with long skirts. Here, a reenactor models a replica shirt.

Although some samples of Viking-age mail are made entirely from riveted rings, most use alternating rows of riveted and solid rings, such as the mail shirt found at Gjermundbu (shown facing the chapter title page).

The orientation of the slag intrusions in the rings of the Gjermundbu mail suggests that the solid rings were punched out of sheet metal, whereas the riveted rings were made from drawn wire. The square cross section of the solid rings

provides further evidence that the rings were punched.

Most samples of Viking-age mail use round rivets, such as the Gjermundbu mail. The smooth, unfaceted shape of the Gjermundbu rivet heads suggests that a setting tool was used to set the rivets.

Some researchers have proposed that the solid rings were made from open rings by welding them closed. The archaeological evidence is

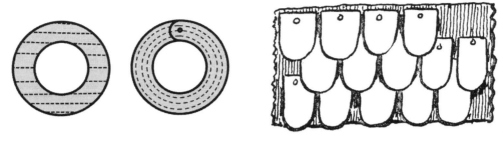

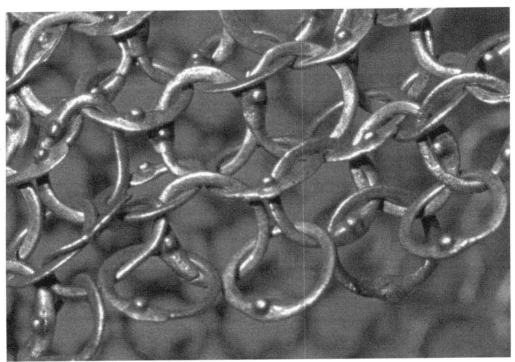

Top left: Slag intrusions (dashed lines) in the iron of the rings of the Gjermundbu mail indicate that the solid rings were punched from sheet metal, while the riveted rings were fabricated from drawn wire. Top right: Scale armor, fabricated from hard plates attached to a backing garment, were used in other lands during the Viking age, but probably not by Vikings. Bottom: This 13th-century mail shirt from the collection of the Higgins Armory Museum was made using very thin wire for the rings. Some Viking-age mail was also made with wire this fine.

slight, but a few samples of mail rings found at Birka in Sweden show some evidence of having been welded.

Regardless of how it was accomplished, the rings of mail used in a shirt were made solid. Links that were simply bent into shape and butted together without a means to hold them shut were not strong enough to withstand the rigors of combat.

The rings were assembled into panels of manageable size and weight, before being linked together to make the final garment. As the panels were linked, alterations to the 4-in-1 pattern were made to shape the fabric to the contours of the body and to provide freedom of motion in places such as the armpit. Rings were dropped or added to rows as needed to shape the finished fabric.

During the Viking age, the diameter and gauge of the wire rings varied considerably. The sleeve of a 13th-century mail shirt, for example, uses finer wire and smaller rings than either the modern reproduction or the Gjermundbu mail. All three, however, are in the range of wire and ring diameters that were used in the Viking age.

The ring diameter in the Gjermundbu shirt averages 8 mm (0.3 in), and the wire diameter averages 1.2 mm (0.05 in, about No. 18 USSW gauge).

In the stories, mail is usually called *brynja*, meaning *mail shirt*. In one case, the word *hringabrynja* (ring mail) is used. Another type of mail is called *spangabrynja*, usually translated as *plate-mail*, such as in chapter 5 of *Grœnlendinga þáttr*. Whatever it might have been, the story says that Símon did not care for it, and he threw it to the ground as useless junk.

One wonders if it might have been scale armor, made from many small overlapping scales of a hard material such as iron or horn attached to a backing garment of leather or fabric.

Although scale armor was not commonly used in Viking lands, it was known in other parts of the world where Vikings traveled, such as Byzantium.

The Bayeux tapestry shows combatants wearing what appears to be mail leggings. They were more commonly used after the Viking age and were called *chausses*. There is no convincing evidence that Vikings wore mail of this type, although it has been suggested that King Harald's mail shirt called Emma was as long as it was because it also included mail leggings.

It is important to note that mail does not provide a complete defense; mail is only a secondary defense. If one were to draw the edge of

An illustration from the Bayeux tapestry shows a warrior wearing mail leggings, which were probably not used by Vikings.

a sword across the arm of a combatant wearing a mail shirt, the sword wouldn't bite, and the mail would protect against the slice. However, if one were to take that same sword and strike a powerful blow against the arm or shoulder of the combatant, the mail would not prevent the skin from being bruised, or the bones from being broken. The mail does little to absorb or dissipate the force of a blow, and the force passes right through.

Before and after the Viking era, fighting men wore padded garments under their mail to help absorb the force of a blow. Typically, these garments consisted of two layers of wool, linen, or leather stuffed with fleece, animal hair, or cloth, then sewn together. There is no archaeological evidence, however, that such garments were worn during the Viking era, nor any mention of them in the stories. In later medieval times, this kind of garment was called a *gambeson*.

The word *herklæði* is used in several instances in the sagas, which has the literal meaning of

A reenactor wears a replica of a padded garment meant to be worn under mail. While combatants in other eras used these padded garments, there is little evidence that Vikings used them.

battle clothing. Based on the way the word is used in the stories, however, it appears to refer to generic battle gear, and more specifically to defensive armor. In chapter 24 of *Víga-Glúms saga*, land travel was especially difficult one year due to snow, so Glúmr Eyjólfsson arranged to have herklæði brought to Hegranessþing by ship, where he expected a fight. The ship sank, and the cargo was lost, making it more difficult for Glúmr to execute his battle plans at the þing.

Chapter 45 of *Brennu-Njáls* saga says that Sigmundr Lambason was wearing a *panzeri* (corselet) when he fought Skarpheðinn Njálsson. Skarpheðinn's axe passed through the panzeri and into Sigmundr's shoulder. The word is a loan word from Latin, and it is thought to mean a padded linen upper garment. Was Sigmundr wearing a gambeson? Probably not. The exact nature of a panzeri is unknown, and the word is used only in this single instance in the *Sagas of Icelanders*. Most likely, its usage here is an anachronism. Scholars generally agree that these kind of padded garments were not known in northern lands until after the Viking age.

Although mail protects against a cut or a slice, the stories say that mail could be punctured by weapons. In chapter 53 of *Egils saga*, Þórólfr Skalla-Grímsson, using two hands, thrust his spear through Earl Hringr's mail shirt, and through the earl as well.

In chapter 37 of *Laxdæla saga*, Eldgrímr tried to buy horses from Þorleikr Höskuldsson, who refused to sell. When Eldgrímr tried to take the horses, Þorleikr's kinsman Hrútr Herjólfsson saw what was going on and intercepted Eldgrímr.

Eldgrímr turned to ride away with the horses. Hrútr raised his *bryntröll* (meaning *mail troll*, and usually translated as *halberd*) and drove it between Eldgrímr's shoulder blades. The halberd split the mail shirt that Eldgrímr wore, and the head of the halberd came out through

Þórir hundr thrust his spear up under King Óláfr's mail shirt at the Battle of Stiklarstaðir in 1030. (*P. N. Arbo, Olav den Helliges fall i slaget på stikkelstad, 1859, Photo © O. Væring Eftf. AS*)

Eldgrímr's chest, killing him. Hrútr was over eighty years old at the time.

There are examples in the sagas where men thrust weapons up under a mail shirt, causing wounds. Chapter 228 of *Óláfs saga helga* tells of the death of King Óláfr inn helgi at the Battle of Stiklarstaðir in the year 1030.

After being wounded in the leg, King Óláfr leaned against a boulder. Þórir hundr (dog) thrust his spear up under the king's mail, piercing him through the belly. Kálfr struck a blow to the king's neck, and the king fell dead.

One might think that mail, being a rare and costly defense, would be used only by the most prominent of men in battle. Yet there are several examples in the sagas of mail being worn by men in the most mundane and unwarlike of circumstances.

In chapter 2 of *Hallfreðar saga*, it is said that after a long night of drinking, Sokki and his

men went up to the loft of the house to retire for the night. Before they could undress, Óttar Þorvaldsson and Ávaldi Ingjaldsson burst in to the house to avenge their fathers' deaths by Sokki. Óttar thrust his sword up under Sokki's mail shirt into his gut, killing him. An interesting aspect of this episode is that Sokki was wearing mail while drinking at night in his farm house. One wonders why he felt a need to wear mail in this situation.

Chapter 21 of *Reykdæla saga og Víga-Skútu* tells the story of Grímr, an outlaw. He went to Þorgeirr Þorkelsson for assistance, who agreed to help him if he would kill Skúta Áskelsson. Grímr accepted the bargain.

Grímr went to Skúta's farm at Skútustaðir and asked Skúta for shelter and protection, which was granted. Grímr was a good guest through the winter. In spring, Grímr and Skúta went to check the fishing nets at Mývatn

After Skúta's mail protected him from a surprise attack by Grímr, Skúta tied Grímr naked to a stake on one of these islands and left him to die there, tormented by thirst, hunger, and biting insects.

(Midge Lake, so called because of the numerous biting insects in the district around the lake that torment visitors to this day). Skúta's shoe came untied. As he bent down to retie it, Grímr lifted his axe and struck a blow to Skúta's shoulder with the axe. However, Skúta was wearing mail underneath his cloak, which protected him from serious injury. Again, one wonders why Skúta felt a need to wear mail while checking his fishing nets.

Skúta grabbed Grímr and forced the truth from him. In retaliation for his treachery, Skúta took Grímr out to one of the islands in Mývatn and left him there, tied naked to a stake. Grímr died there, tormented by hunger and insect bites.

During the Viking age, fighting men used improvised defenses, and occasionally, they were protected by items that were never intended to be used for defense. Here at Geirvör in west Iceland, a treacherous attack to Snorri goði's arm was blocked by his arm-ring.

6

OTHER PERSONAL DEFENSES IN THE VIKING AGE

The sagas mention other personal defenses. In chapter 45 of *Eyrbyggja saga*, Freysteinn bófi was protected from a sword cut to his neck by a piece of horn sewn into his felt hat. In chapter 41 of *Vatnsdæla saga*, Ingólfr þorsteinsson put flat stones on his chest and back, which protected him when he attacked a band of thieves.

Similarly, Brodd-Helgi þorgilsson protected himself with flat stones under his clothing, described in chapter 2 of *Vopnfirðinga saga*. When Svartr thrust at Brodd-Helgi with his *höggspjót* (halberd), it glanced off the stone so violently that Svartr pitched forward, allowing Brodd-Helgi to cut off his leg. The event took place on Smjörvatnsheiði below Smjörfjöll in Iceland.

Occasionally, objects worn on the body provided protection from an attack, even though they were never intended to serve as armor. In chapter 58 of *Eyrbyggja saga*, Óspakr Kjallaksson and þórir Gull-Harðarson were fighting. þórir lunged at Óspakr with his *bjarnsviðu* (bear knife), but Óspakr avoided the attack. þórir overcommitted and fell forward on his knees, with his head down. Óspakr drove his axe into þórir's back. However, þórir had another knife hanging from a strap around his neck. The knife had slipped around to his back, and it took the force of the blow. þórir received only a slight wound on either side of the knife.

In chapter 44 of *Eyrbyggja saga*, Snorri goði þorgrímsson and his men fought against Steinþórr þorláksson and his men at Geirvör in Álftafjörður in west Iceland, shown opposite.

Snorri requested a truce from Steinþórr's people, and Steinþórr asked Snorri to extend a hand, presumably to seal the truce with a handshake. However, Steinþórr treacherously cut at Snorri's outstretched arm with his sword. The sword landed on the temple ring that Snorri wore on his arm. Snorri was unhurt, but the ring was nearly broken in two.

Icelandic law required that every heathen temple have a silver arm ring weighing at least two ounces, which was used for the swearing of oaths and which the goði was required to wear at certain times. It was probably this ring that Snorri goði wore on his arm.

In chapter 11 of *Grettis saga*, þorgeirr Önundarson walked to the boat shed at Reykjarfjörður before dawn to prepare for a day of fishing. In the dark, þorfinnr came up behind him and drove his axe into þorgeirr's back so that it sank in between his shoulder blades. þorfinnr released the axe and ran away.

What þorfinnr didn't see was that þorgeirr had a leather flask full of drink on his back, which took the full force of the axe blow. The flask was ruined, but þorgeirr was unharmed.

þorgeirr was given the nickname *flöskubakr* (bottle-back). When he next met þorfinnr, he said, "I'm returning your axe," and lopped off þorfinnr's head with the axe.

Top: Brodd-Helgi fought Svartr at Smjörvatnsheiði in east Iceland. Brodd-Helgi protected himself with flat stones under his clothing, so that when Svartr's thrust glanced off the protective stones, Brodd-Helgi was able cut off Svartr's leg. Middle: Þorfinnr attacked Þorgeirr's back at the boathouse of the farm at Reykjarfjörður in west Iceland, shown as it appears today. The attack was blocked by a leather flask full of drink on Þorgeirr's back. Bottom: After pursuing each other through the Böðvarsdalur valley in east Iceland, Bjarni, Þorkell, and their men fought until women from the farm at Eyvindarstaðir threw clothing over the men's weapons to stop the fight.

The stories describe ways in which fights were stopped by third parties. The most common method was to throw clothing or blankets onto the combatants' weapons, rendering them ineffectual. This was done by men to capture an opponent without harming him, as told in chapter 46 of *Egils saga*. Egill and Þórólfr Skalla-Grímsson were raiding in Kúrland on the Baltic Sea. At one farm, Egill and his men met fierce resistance. The Kúrlanders forced Egill's band into a cul-de-sac in a stockade, and then rendered them harmless by throwing clothing over their weapons. The prisoners were bound and locked into an outbuilding for the night, so they could be killed one by one the next day. That night, Egill and his men were able to slip their bonds and escape.

In a similar manner, clothing was used by women to stop a fight, as told in chapter 18 of *Vopnfirðinga saga*. Þorkell Geitisson and his men were pursuing Bjarni Brodd-Helgason and his men down from the heath and through the Böðvarsdalur Valley. They caught up with one another at the farm called Eyvindarstaðir.

A fierce battle broke out. A woman on the farm saw the fight and ran to tell the farmer, Eyvindr. He decided to stop this fight between kinsmen. He grabbed a large wooden beam, and he told the women to bring clothing. Eyvindr waded between the two sides swinging the wooden beam, while the women threw clothing on the combatants' weapons making them useless.

In another case, clothing was thrown on weapons by an unarmed man while under attack. In chapter 39 of *Finnboga saga ramma*, Þorgrímr was sent to the farm Finnbogastaðir as an assassin. When he arrived, he asked the farmer, Finnbogi Ásbjarnarson, for work.

Finnbogi gave him the task of building walls to enclose the hayfields. One day, when Finnbogi went out to inspect Þorgrímr's work,

The leather flask that protected Þorgeirr's back at Reykjarfjörður might have resembled this modern replica.

he was overcome with fatigue. He sat down against a wall with his cloak around his head and fell asleep.

Þorgrímr pulled out a hidden sword and made to strike Finnbogi, but the farmer was not as soundly asleep as he seemed. Finnbogi threw his cloak over the sword to reduce its effectiveness, and then he grappled with Þorgrímr, bringing him down. Þorgrímr admitted that he was sent by Jökull Ingimundarson to kill Finnbogi and asked for quarter. Finnbogi said the only request he was willing to grant was an end to their dealings, and he chopped off Þorgrímr's head with the sword.

Replica Viking-age axes show some of the distinctive styles in use during the Viking age.

7

BATTLE AXES

WHEN people think of Viking-age weapons, they usually think first of the battle axe, and the image that forms in their mind is a massive weapon that only a troll could wield.

In reality, battle axes in the Viking age were light, fast, well balanced, and were good for speedy, deadly attacks, as well as for a variety of nasty tricks.

The axe was often the choice of the poorest man in the Viking age. Even the lowliest farm had to have a wood axe for cutting and splitting wood. In desperation, a poor man could pick up the farm axe and use it in a fight.

Axes meant for battle were designed a bit differently than farm axes. The photo on the facing page shows two reproduction axes based on 10th-century finds.

A wide variety of axe-head shapes were used in the Viking age. In the early part of the Viking era, the cutting edge was generally 7 to 15 cm (3 to 6 in) long, whereas later, axes became much larger, with crescent-shaped edges 22 to 45 cm (9 to 18 in) long. These axes were called *breið-øx* (broad axe).

Large axe heads are also known from saga sources. In chapter 80 of *Egils saga*, it is said that Steinarr Önundarson gave his slave þrándr an axe whose head was nearly one *alin* long, the length from the elbow to the end of the longest finger. Along with the axe, Steinarr gave his slave orders that guaranteed the wrath and retaliation of þorsteinn Egilsson. The large axe did not help þrándr. þorsteinn made short work of the slave using the small axe he carried.

Axe heads were made of iron and were single edged. Some axes used a hardened steel edge welded to the iron head. The steel permitted the axe to hold a better edge than iron would have allowed.

Some axe heads were elaborately decorated with inlays of precious metals, notably the axe head found in Mammen, Denmark. The head is decorated on every flat surface with inlays of gold and silver and was found in a rich grave that dates from the year 971.

Perhaps the most famous axe in the sagas is *Rimmugýgr* (Battle Ogre) carried by Skarpheðinn Njálsson in *Brennu-Njáls saga*. There's little in the way of physical description of the axe in the saga, but in the hands of Skarpheðinn, it was clearly a powerful and trusty weapon. When Skarpheðinn taunted þorkell þorgeirsson at Alþing, described in chapter 120, Skarpheðinn stood grinning, with his axe at the ready, and offered to split þorkell in two down to his shoulders, saying, "I've never lifted my weapon against any man without its hitting its mark."

Typically, the axe head had a wedge-shaped cross section, tapering toward the edge.

Top: These historical wood axes date from the modern era, but virtually identical axes were in use on Viking-age farms. Bottom left: These three Viking-age axe heads are from a private collection and show a range of representative shapes. Bottom right: The larger of these Viking age axe heads is approximately 22 cm (9 in) long.

The cross section of the head near the edge was sometimes diamond shaped, which provided for greater strength for a given weight of iron.

Chapter 23 of *Fóstbræðra saga* tells of a special axe made by Bjarni for Þormóðr Bersason, which was hammered all the way out to the edge with no obstructions, resulting in a very sharp blade. Perhaps that blade had the very thin, elegant cross section, seen on many historical examples resulting in a lightweight and speedy axe. A blade on this type of axe would be too thin and delicate for splitting wood; this axe was meant for splitting skulls.

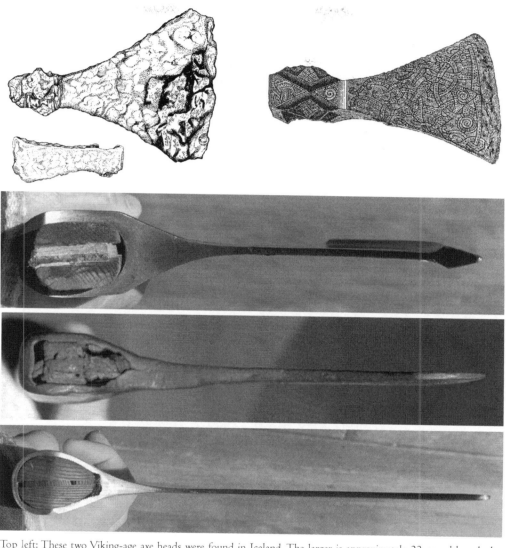

Top left: These two Viking-age axe heads were found in Iceland. The larger is approximately 22 cm, although the "horns" at the tips have broken off. (*Michéle Hayeur-Smith, Fornleifastofnun Íslands*) Top right: The 10th-century axe head found at Mammen in Denmark is richly decorated with silver and gold inlay. Middle: The cross sections of three axe heads are compared. At the top is a replica axe head, showing the diamond cross section of the head near the edge, providing additional strength. In the middle is a 12th-century axe head from the collection of the Higgins Armory Museum. It has a thin, elegant head, making for a speedy and light-weight axe. At the bottom is a replica axe head having the same thin, elegant cross section as the historical axe head.

Thick, wedge-shaped axe heads were made as a single piece, with the eye (the hole for the haft) punched out with a drift.

The thinner blades show evidence of having been folded around what would eventually become the eye before being welded into a solid unit.

I am not aware of any archaeological evidence for double-edged axe heads in the Viking age, nor of any mention of them in the stories.

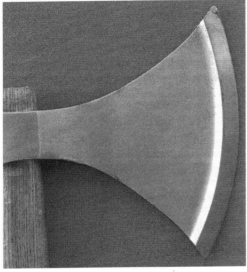

Above: This Viking-age axe head from a private collection was fabricated by folding thin iron around what would become the eye for the haft and then welding the layers of iron together. Left: This replica axe head has a diamond-shaped cross section near the edge of the head for extra strength.

Some translators use *double-bladed axe* for the word *bryntröll*, but I believe that usage is speculative. As discussed in more detail in the chapter on other offensive weapons, it is not known what sort of weapon that *bryntröll* refers to. In chapter 2 of *Valla-Ljóts saga*, it is said that Ljótr Ljótólfsson carried a *bryntröll* when he was in a good mood. When he was in a killing mood, he carried a *snaghyrnd öx* (snag-horned axe).

The sagas contain many examples of axe heads that shattered in use, usually when they struck stones. Skalla-Grímr Kveld-Úlfsson was given a fabulous axe by King Eiríkr blóðøx (blood axe) as is told in chapter 38 of *Egils saga*. It was inlaid with gold and plated with silver. The gift may have been none too welcome because the king's father had driven Skalla-

Grímr and his father out of Norway. Skalla-Grímr used it to slaughter two oxen simultaneously. The axe went right through the oxen's necks and hit a stone, shattering the edge, which may have been the result that Skalla-Grímr was expecting. He placed the shattered axe in the rafters of his longhouse where smoke and dampness could finish the job of ruining the axe.

Chapter 11 of *Eiríks saga rauða* tells of some American Indians who found a Viking iron axe beside the body of one of Þorfinnr karlsefni's men in Vínland. The axe would have been a complete novelty to the Indians who were unfamiliar with working or using iron. They took turns chopping at a tree with the axe and thought it was a treasure. But when the axe hit a stone and shattered, they threw it away as worthless junk. *Grænlendinga saga* enhances the story a bit by saying the natives tested the axe against the head of one of their fellows.

The pointed "horns" at each end of the blade (*öxarhyrna*) were kept sharp so they could be used offensively, as was done by Kolbeinn Þorljótsson in chapter 5 of *Grænlendinga þáttr*. He drove the horn of his axe into Þórðr's

Above: A replica axe is shown being used in a manner similar to a bottle opener to capture the opponent's shield rim, allowing the shield to be wrenched away. Right: These two replica axes illustrate the difference in the length of the haft for a one-handed (left) and two-handed (right) axe.

throat, killing him. The horns can also be used for slashing attacks, such as across the belly.

It is possible that the snag-horned axe carried by Ljótr Ljótólfsson in *Valla-Ljóts saga* had a horn fashioned as a hook to make these kinds of slashing attacks even more deadly.

The shape of some axe heads allow them to be used in a manner reminiscent of modern, but now nearly obsolete, bottle openers. Once the edge of the shield is captured in the axe head, the head hooks the shield and captures it firmly. The combatant holding the axe has tremendous leverage on the shield and can control it and force it from the hands of his opponent at will while menacing his opponent with the edge and horns of the axe.

The axe haft was made of wood such as ash and was as long as 1.5 m (60 in). The haft was sized for the intended use of the axe and to balance the axe head. Axes with smaller heads had shorter hafts and were used one handed, whereas longer hafted weapons were used two handed. Both of the reproduction axes shown here are nicely balanced, despite the significant difference in the lengths of their hafts.

It is possible that much longer axe hafts were used, which could reach over the heads of the men in front ranks in a mass battle to attack the opposing line from a rank in the rear. Evidence for such long hafts is slight.

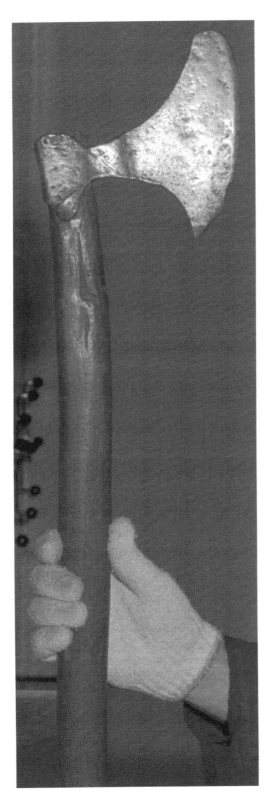

AT one time, my opinion was that the axe, being poorly balanced, was harder to control than a well-balanced weapon like a sword. However, some hands-on experiences have forced me to change my opinion.

One advantage of an axe over other edged weapons is that all the force of the blow is concentrated into a small section of the blade, so the axe has enough power to punch through a helmet or mail.

Little is known of the details of combat techniques used by Vikings when they fought with axes.

Many of the later medieval combat manuals teach the use of the halberd, the pollaxe, and other staff weapons. These techniques do not translate well to Viking axes. For example, most of the parrying techniques from the manuals are not directly applicable to Viking axes, yet we know from the sagas that axes were routinely used to defend against incoming blows.

In chapter 21 of *Fljótsdæla saga*, þorkell Eyjólfsson drew his sword and struck at Gunnarr þiðrandabani, who raised his axe over his head to parry. The sword hit the axehead so firmly that it stuck fast. Gunnarr raised the axe further to stop the fight. In chapter 16 of *Króka-Refs saga*, Narfi thrust repeatedly with his spear at Grani, who had an axe in his hand. Grani parried the thrusts with his axe, but eventually Narfi ran him through. Narfi dragged the body away and covered it while Grani was still in his death throes.

A 12th-century axe from the collection of the Higgins Armory Museum weighs a total of only 770 g (1.7 lb.), making for a light-weight, well-balanced, fast, and brutally effective weapon. It is hard to claim that a Viking-age axe requires the strength of a troll after experiencing something as fast and light as this example.

Top: Meyer's combat treatise of 1570 teaches techniques for the halberd. (*Higgins Armory Museum*) Bottom: Talhoffer's treatise of 1467 teaches techniques for the pollaxe. Some of the techniques for polearms taught in these later manuals are applicable to the Viking axe, but many are not.

To date, our best results have come from applying some of the sword and shield techniques to the one-handed axe. The sword and the one-handed axe have similar reach, and many tricks described in the chapter on sword and shield technique are directly applicable.

However, this approach fails to take advantage of the shape of the axe head, and as a result, we miss many of the hooking, pulling, and wrenching tricks that are clearly possible with an axe.

For example, the curved shape of the head allows the axe to hook an opponent's ankle, throwing him off balance and onto the ground.

The identical trick shows up in later combat manuals, such as Meyer, using the halberd. The trick is also taught using other weapons, such as the longsword, hooking the opponent with the crossguard, the wide bar adjacent to the grip of a longsword that serves to protect the hand.

Meyer and others teach that the axe head can be hooked over other body parts, such as the

Above left: The sword and the one-handed axe have similar reach. Above right: Because of their similar reach, many of the tricks for the sword seem directly applicable to the one-handed axe. Left: The axe head can be used to hook body parts, such as the ankle to throw an opponent off balance and onto the ground.

neck, to compel a person to move in a direction he doesn't wish to go.

These kinds of hooking tricks are described in the sagas, too. Chapter 21 of *Sturlu saga* tells how Þorsteinn Tjörvason hooked one of Sturla's men with his axe and dragged him over to where he could be stabbed.

The later combat manuals teach that the butt end of long-hafted weapons can be used offen-

sively. Some of these tricks seem directly applicable to the Viking axe.

When two combatants have closed the distance, it is possible to strike or wrench with the butt of the haft, simultaneously defending against the opponent's attack, as shown in Meyer. Although an attack with the butt end is not likely to be lethal, it is certainly likely to distract an opponent.

Top: Meyer's manual of 1570 teaches using a halberd to hook and catch an opponent's ankle. Bottom: Meyer also teaches the hooking of other body parts, tricks that work well with the Viking axe. (*Higgins Armory Museum*)

One defensive trick from the later manuals that works very well with a two-handed Viking axe is to use the haft for an overhead parry. Meyer shows a technique with a halberd haft that is directly applicable to two-handed Viking axes and is illustrated on the following page. The opponent on the left has positioned the haft of his halberd over his head to protect against the combatant's overhead attack.

Many sorts of incoming blows can be parried or set aside by the axe haft using this kind of technique. The effectiveness of these techniques make it quite believable that þormóðr Bersason could say in chapter 24 of *Fóstbrœðra saga* that his axe would serve as his shield and his mail shirt.

An example of this kind of trick with a two-handed Viking axe is demonstrated in the sequence of photographs beginning on page 81 and continuing to the following page.

A, the combatant on the right, has reversed his axe to shorten his grip and has caught **B**'s

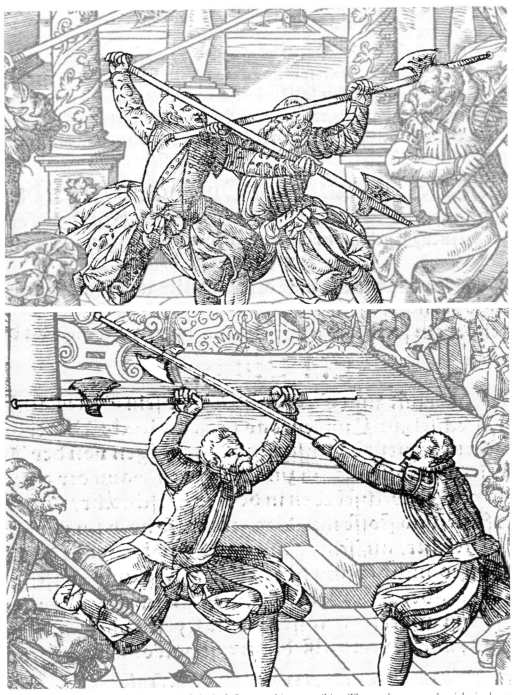

Top: Meyer teaches using the butt end of the haft for wrenching or striking. The combatant on the right is about to cast his opponent down, a trick that can be applied to a Viking axe as well. Bottom: The haft can be used for parrying, as is being demonstrated by the combatant on the left in Meyer's manual. (*Higgins Armory Museum*)

A DEMONSTRATION OF A DEFENSIVE TECHNIQUE WITH THE TWO-HANDED AXE. **A**, the combatant on the right, parries **B**'s overhead attack with his axe haft.

high attack with an overhead parry. **A** then slides his axe backwards to catch and hook **B**'s axe head. This move increases **A**'s leverage, and it prevents **B** from easily disengaging.

A wrenches **B**'s axe away and to the side. The leverage makes it possible to pull the axe right out of **B**'s hands.

If **B** does not let go, his body flies forward with his axe, directly onto the butt end of **A**'s axe. The blow is not likely to be lethal to **B**, but, as the saga authors often say about this kind of attack, neither is it likely to improve **B**'s appearance any. **A** can follow up with a variety of attacks with the edge or haft of his axe.

As with any of the combat sequences demonstrated in this text, many counterattacks are possible. For example, as **A** wrenches **B**'s axe, **B** has an opportunity to attack **A**'s exposed side with his shield. However, **A**'s wrench and thrust come so quickly that **B** has little time to execute his counterattack.

Other stories in the sagas suggest that one would not want to catch the edge of a weapon on an axe haft for fear that the haft would break. In chapter 58 of *Eyrbyggja saga*, Óspakr Kjallaksson parried a sword blow with his axe. The blow struck the haft, shattering it so that the axe head fell to the ground.

Some hafted weapons are described in the sagas as having iron reinforcements on the haft, perhaps to reduce the risk of breaking the haft while parrying or while executing other techniques that stress the haft. The historical axe shown on page 83 has such reinforcements on two surfaces of the haft.

In chapter 11 of *Brennu-Njáls saga*, it is said that Þjóstólfr had a large axe with an iron-wrapped haft, which he used to kill Þorvaldr

Top: Continuing the sequence, **A** hooks **B**'s axe head and carries it off to the side, neutralizing any threat from **B**'s axe. **A** has enough leverage to pull **B**'s axe out of his hands. Bottom: **A** is also in a good position to drive the butt of his axe into **B**'s face.

Top left: This historical axe from a private collection has iron reinforcements on the haft. Bottom left: Meyer teaches that when the blade of the longsword goes low, the hilt should be held high to protect the head. (*Higgins Armory Museum*) Right: That seems like good advice for the two-handed axe, which, like the longsword, is used simultaneously for both offense and defense.

Ósvífrsson, the husband of Hallgerðr Höskuldsdóttir. When þjóstólfr returned to Hallgerðr, who was also þjóstólfr's foster daughter, she asked him what had happened to make his axe all bloody. He replied, "That which will allow you to be married a second time."

Meyer teaches that whenever the blade of the longsword goes low, the hilt should be raised, to protect the head, as shown in the illustration from his manual above. That seems to be good advice for the two-handed axe, which, like the longsword, is used simultaneously for offense and defense.

Raising the butt end of the axe to cover the head when the axe head goes low provides significant protection against a counterattack to the head.

The later manuals teach techniques used from the bind, a state of engagement where the combatant has attacked and the opponent has defended, and where the weapons remain in contact. Some of these techniques are applicable to the Viking axe.

A two-handed axe can be reversed in the hands, as taught by Talhoffer for the pollaxe in the illustration on the next page. It is a quick way to increase the available length of the haft, which can be use for thrusting or wrenching.

A high attack with an axe, especially one that's been telegraphed, can be defeated by running in under the attack. By closing the distance, the opponent is out of range of the attack. He is simply too close for the axe to be a threat. The opponent can attack the combatant with his

A long-hafted weapon can be reversed in the hands, as illustrated in Talhoffer's manual of 1467, increasing the effective length of the haft. The combatant on the left has reversed his pollaxe and is using the haft to throw his opponent to the ground.

shield, or his weapon, or simply grapple, which is exactly what Björn Hítdœlakappi did in chapter 19 of *Bjarnar saga Hítdœlakappa*. Björn suspected that Þorsteinn Kálfsson had come as an assassin. When Þorsteinn raised his axe, Björn run under the attack to grapple. He threw Þorsteinn down, knocking the wind out of him, and then Björn strangled him.

Axes, as well as other weapons, were sometimes used to strike blows that were not intended to be lethal. The *öxarhamar* (axe hammer), the backside of the axe head, was used for that purpose. Sometimes, the blow was made to humiliate an opponent, or in other cases, was made against an opponent so inferior that he didn't seem worthy of a proper blow. In chapter 9 of *Þórðar saga hreðu*, Özurr Árngrímsson and his men surrounded the cowardly Þórhallr and forced him to betray the location of his friend, Þórðr Þórðarson. Özurr struck at Þórhallr with the hammer of his axe, knocking him out, and said, "It's bad to have a slave as your best friend."

In several cases in the sagas, the axe hammer was used to strike an unintended but lethal blow. In chapter 146 of *Brennu-Njáls saga*,

Þorgeirr Þórisson rushed to attack Þorkell Sigfússon, but as he did so, another man came at Þorgeirr from behind. As Þorgeirr raised his axe in the backswing, the axe hammer struck the man behind on the skull, killing him. With the forward swing, Þorgeirr chopped off one of Þorkell's arms at the shoulder.

In chapter 16 of *Ljósvetninga saga*, a story is told of the use of an axe where a more suitable tool might have served better. When he was young, Guðmundr Eyjólfsson used his hand to wave mosquitoes off the bald spot on his foster father's head while the old man napped outside. His brother Einarr Eyjólfsson suggested Guðmundr use his axe, instead, to drive the mosquitoes away. Guðmundr took the advice, drawing blood from the old man's head. Only then did Guðmundr realize that Einarr's advice was not well intended. The bad feelings between the brothers continued into later life.

It's not clear if axes were routinely used as throwing weapons. One of the few examples from the sagas where an axe was thrown is in chapter 33 of *Harðar saga*. In a battle, Þorvaldr bláskeggr (black beard) drove a spear through Sigurðr Gunnhildarson, who had been fighting with an axe. Sigurðr threw his axe at Þorvaldr, hitting him in the head. They both fell down dead. The sense of the story is that the axe was Sigurðr's normal battle axe, rather than a specialized throwing axe.

The battle at Stiklarstaðir in Norway, which occurred on July 29, 1030, was a massive dynastic battle involving more than 14,000 combatants. Chapter 226 of *Óláfs saga helga* says that men in the front rank used their swords, whereas those in the next rank thrust with their spears. Men in the rear shot arrows and spears and threw stones and hand-axes (*handöx*) at the opposite side.

One recovered historic axe head resembles Frankish throwing axes that predate the Viking

Above: A historical axe head from a private collection that resembles Frankish throwing axes. Perhaps Vikings used similar throwing axes, but there's little evidence to support the conjecture. Right: The Bayeux tapestry shows combatants using their two-handed axes left-handed so that their blows come in on the undefended side of an opponent with a shield.

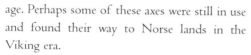

age. Perhaps some of these axes were still in use and found their way to Norse lands in the Viking era.

Another trick with an axe is described in chapter 62 of *Eyrbyggja saga*. Outlaws living at the farm at Eyrr fortified it. The nature of the fortification (*virki*) is not certain, but it probably took the form of a tall stockade fence. Snorri goði and his men attacked the outlaws in their stronghold. Þrándr Ingjaldsson leapt up and hooked the head of his axe over the wall of the fortification. He pulled himself by his axe handle into the fortification and attacked Hrafn, cutting off Hrafn's arm with his axe.

Images from the Bayeux tapestry show combatants using their axes two handed, but left handed. Thus, the blows come in on the undefended sides of their opponents.

This same technique is also taught in the later combat treatises.

One wonders whether men used sheaths on their axes in the Viking age to protect against accidental cuts. There is no archaeological evidence to suggest their use, and the little available literary evidence suggests they were not used. In chapter 144 of *Íslendinga saga*, which takes place well after the Viking age, it is said

that an unnamed man was accidentally wounded by an axe as men mounted their horses to ride to a killing in west Iceland. The episode suggests that the head of the axe was not covered.

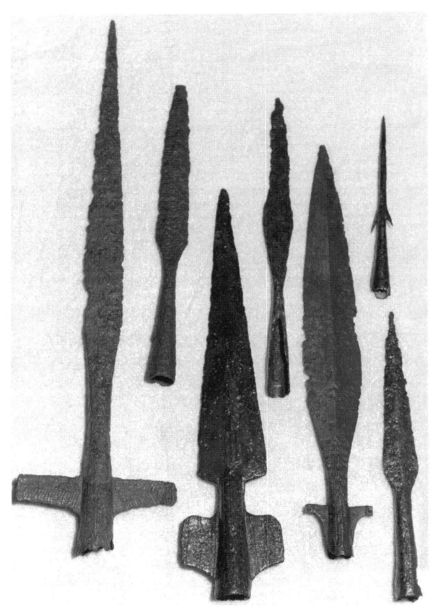

Viking-age spearheads came in a wide variety of sizes and shapes. This assortment of historical Viking-age spearheads is from a private collection.

8

SPEARS

THE spear was the most commonly used weapon in the Viking age. It was often the choice of someone who was unable to afford a sword. During the Viking age, spears were made of iron heads affixed to long wooden shafts. Spearheads took many forms.

The photo on the facing page shows seven historical spearheads from the Viking age, illustrating the variations in size and shape that existed during the period. Earlier spearheads were about 20 cm (8 in) long, whereas later ones were as long as 60 cm (24 in). The short barbed spearhead in the upper right is 20 cm (8 in) long, whereas the triangular-shaped spearhead in the center is 38 cm (15 in) long.

In chapter 55 of *Laxdæla saga*, Helgi Harðbeinsson had a spear with a blade one *ell* long (about 50 cm, or 20 in). He thrust the blade through Bolli Þorleiksson's shield, and through Bolli.

Some spearheads had "wings" or "ears" on the heads. Besides limiting the depth of penetration in a thrust, the wings could be used to catch and hook the opponent's weapons and for other tricks. In chapter 10 of *Þorskfirðinga saga*, Askmaðr inn þungi (the heavy) tried to snag Már Hallvarðsson's shield away from him using his spear (*króksvíða*).

Spearheads were made of iron. They were sometimes made using pattern-welding techniques, which create the herringbone pattern seen on the surface of some historical spearheads. (The technique of pattern-welding is described in more detail in the chapter on swords.)

Spearheads were frequently decorated with inlays of precious metals or with scribed geometric designs.

In cross section, spearheads were lozenge shaped, with a thick central rib. The head tapered smoothly to a sharp edge on either side of the rib.

After forming the head, the smith flattened and drew out material to form the socket. This material was formed around a mandrel and, in many cases, was welded to form a solid socket. In some cases, the overlapping portions of the socket were left unwelded.

The wings were formed separately and then welded to the socket. The sockets on the surviving spearheads suggest that the shafts were typically round, with a diameter of 2 to 3 cm (about 1 in). However, there is little evidence that tells us the length of the shaft. The archaeological evidence is negligible, and the sagas are, for the most part, silent. Chapter 6 of *Gísla saga* tells of a spear so long shafted that a man's outstretched arm could touch the rivet holding the head on the shaft. The language used suggests that such a long shaft was uncommon.

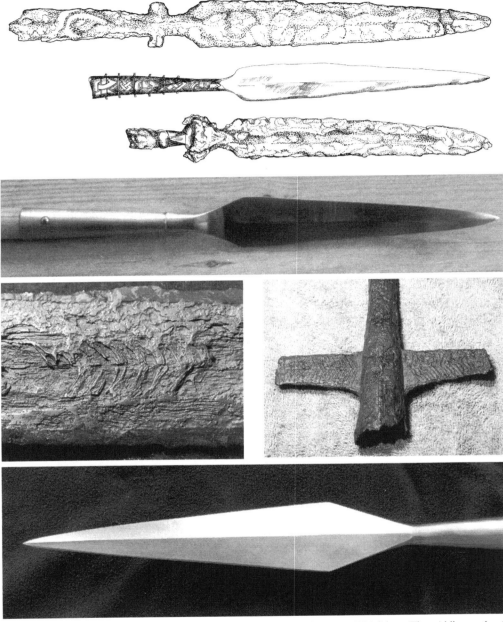

Top: The longest of these three Viking-age spearheads found in Iceland is 33cm (13 in) long. The middle spearhead is a splendid piece of artistry, decorated with protruding nail heads and inlaid with niello, a black alloy of sulfur, copper, silver, and lead. (*Illustration: Michéle Hayeur-Smith, Fornleifastofnun Íslands*) Middle: This replica spearhead is typical of those used late in the Viking age, when spearheads became much longer. Middle left: Some spearheads were made using pattern-welding techniques, discussed in more detail on the chapter on swords. Middle right: Spearheads were frequently decorated. This Viking-age spearhead from a private collection uses scribed geometric designs on the wings. Bottom: The lozenge-shaped cross section of a Viking spearhead is clearly visible in this modern replica.

Above: The wings on the spearheads were formed separately and then welded to the socket, as seen on this Viking-age example from a private collection. Right: While surviving spearheads tell us the diameter of Viking-age spear shafts, there is little evidence that tells us about their length. Gísla saga tells of a spear so long-shafted that a man's outstretched arm could touch the rivet holding the head to the shaft.

Reproduction spears have been made with shorter and longer shafts. First impressions formed while working with reproduction spears having various shaft lengths suggest that the shorter spear is a speedier, better balanced weapon.

However, the later medieval combat manuals teach techniques for extremely long-hafted pole weapons that result in speedy tricks, some of which seem to apply very well to long Viking-age spears.

Perhaps the best guess we can make is that the combined length of shaft and head of Viking-age spears was 2 to 3m (7 to 10 ft) long, although one can make arguments for the use of spears having longer and shorter shafts. A strong, straight-grained wood such as ash was used for the shaft.

Meyer and other medieval combat manuals teach speedy tricks for long-hafted pole weapons, some of which apply to long-shafted Viking-age spears. (*Higgins Armory Museum*)

Whatever the typical shaft length might have been, a story from chapter 15 of *Fóstbrœðra saga* suggests that the amount of wood was not insubstantial. Gautr Sleituson's men ran out of firewood while cooking their meal. Gautr took Þorgeirr Hávarsson's spear and shield from his tent and broke them up, which provided firewood sufficient to cook the meal. Þorgeirr seemed unperturbed when he returned to the camp and discovered his weapons were missing, but he later returned the favor by using his axe to split Gautr apart down to his shoulders.

There are examples in the sagas of spear shafts reinforced with iron. In chapter 40 of *Vatnsdæla saga*, it is said that Ingólfr Þorsteinsson's spear had a broad blade and a shaft reinforced with iron. As with an axe haft, the reinforcements reduced the risk that the shaft would break when stressed or when parrying an edged weapon.

In other historical periods, the butt end of the spear shaft was covered with a metal butt cap, to help protect the wooden shaft and to help balance the weapon. The evidence for the use of these caps in the Viking age is very slight, so if they were used, they were not common.

A spearhead was fixed to its wooden shaft using a rivet. The rivets are surprisingly small. The rivet head on the historical spearhead illustrated on the facing page has survived nearly intact, visible below the wing. The rivet head diameter is a little over 3 mm (1/8 in).

A passage from chapter 48 of *Grettis saga* suggests that the rivet could easily be removed. Grettir Ásmundarson arrived at Þorbjörn Arnórsson's farm, Þoroddsstaðir, to take revenge on Þorbjörn for his killing of Grettir's brother, Atli Ásmundarson. After Grettir arrived at the farm, he sat down and removed the rivet from his spear to prevent Þorbjörn from throwing it back at him should the spear miss its target. Grettir was able to take out the rivet with nothing more than the tools he carried on his person, most likely his belt knife, which suggests that however the rivet may have been set, it was not very robust.

When Grettir threw the spear, the spearhead flew off, and it missed its mark. After killing

Left: The spearhead was fixed to the shaft with a small rivet, which has survived just below the wing on this historical Viking-age spearhead from a private collection. Right: Grettir traveled to the farm of Þoroddsstaðir, shown as it appears today, to avenge his brother's death. On arrival, he sat down and removed the rivet from his spear, lest it should be thrown back at him during the fight.

Þorbjörn and his son, Grettir searched for the spearhead but couldn't find it.

According to the saga, the spearhead was found in the marshland behind the farm centuries later. The saga author says that people alive at the time the saga was written could remember the spearhead being found.

In chapter 13 of *Gísla saga*, Vésteinn Vésteinsson was killed by an assassin in the night using the spear Grásíða. The murderer left the spear in the wound, turning the simple manslaughter into the more horrific crime known as *morð* (secret murder), according to the saga author. Gísli drew the spear from the wound and tossed it, covered in blood, into a chest, so that no one else in the house would have to see it.

The chest would have to have been extremely large to contain a spearhead on a shaft. Even though the saga is silent on the matter, I wonder if Gísli first removed the head from the shaft before throwing the bloody spearhead into the chest.

Many people think of the spear primarily as a projectile: a weapon that is thrown through the air. One of the Norse myths tells the story of the first battle in the world, in which Óðinn, the highest of the gods, threw a spear over the heads of the opposing combatants as a prelude to the fight.

The sagas say that spears were also thrown in this manner when men, rather than gods, fought. At the battle at Geirvör described in chapter 44 of *Eyrbyggja saga*, the saga author says that Steinþórr Þorláksson threw a spear over the heads of Snorri goði and his men according to the old custom, to bring good luck. The spear found a target, putting Már Hallvarðsson out of the fight. Snorri goði dryly observed, "It's not always best to walk last."

Although spears were certainly used as projectiles during the Viking age, there's a disadvantage to throwing your weapon away in a fight. Not only do you lose your weapon, but you also risk having your opponent pick it up and use it against you if you miss. Worse, your weapon may be caught in flight and flung back at you, a trick used on several occasions by Gunnarr Hámundarson, such as in chapter 54 of *Brennu-Njáls saga*. Gunnarr fought against Otkell Skarfsson and his men. Auðólfr threw a spear at Gunnarr, who caught it in the air and sent it back to Auðólfr. The spear penetrated Auðólfr's shield and Auðólfr.

Despite these risks, the sagas are filled with examples where spears were thrown to attack an opponent from a distance. In sea battles, spears and other projectiles were routinely shot between ships. During the Battle of Svölðr, the shower of spears and arrows launched against King Óláfr Tryggvason's ship was so thick that his men could hardly protect themselves with their shields, as described in chapter 107 of *Óláfs saga Tryggvasonar*.

Spears were also used with "throwing strings" (*snærisspjót*) for longer reach. Although the details of the use of these strings are not known, it is likely that they served to impart greater velocity to the spear at the instant of release. Devices having the same goal of increasing the velocity of the missile at the moment of release have been used by many cultures from prehistoric to modern times. Notable among these devices is the atlatl, but there is no evidence that Viking snærisspjót resembled the atlatl.

In chapter 24 of *Reykdæla saga og Víga-Skútu*, Skúta Áskelsson was on one side of the river ford at Eyjarvað with his men, and Glúmr Eyjólfsson and Eyjólfr Einarsson and their men were on the other side. Both sides had a quarrel to settle with the other. Skúta shot a spear across the river with throwing strings, killing þrándr, which put both sides on notice that the quarrel was going to be a bloody one.

More commonly, the spear was used as a thrusting weapon. It provided a means to inflict injuries from a distance.

This capability was used to advantage in mass battles. Vikings tended to avoid mass battles, however, and preferred the mêlée. They were at a disadvantage against the trained, disciplined troops that were being built up in other European lands of the time. However, if a mass battle were necessary, men lined up, shoulder to shoulder, with shields overlapping. After all the preliminaries, which included rock throwing, name calling, the trading of insults, and shouting a war cry (*æpa heróp*), the two lines advanced toward each other. When the lines met, the battle was begun. Behind the wall of shields, each line was well protected. Once a line was broken, and one side could pass through the line of the other side, terrible damage could be done from behind. The battle usually then broke down into armed mêlées between small groups of men.

Before either line broke, while the two lines were going at each other hammer and tongs, the spear offered some real advantages. A fighter in the second rank could use his spear to reach over the heads of his comrades in the first rank and attack the opposing line. *Konungs skuggsjá* (*King's Mirror*), a 13th-century Norwegian manual for men of the king, says that in the battle line a spear is more effective than two swords.

When the line broke, stories say that people would sling their shields over their shoulders and use the spear two handed, as done by þórólfr Skalla-Grímsson in chapter 53 of *Egils saga*. During a battle in the service of King Aðalsteinn of England, þórólfr fought furiously, holding the spear two handed with his shield on his back. He hacked and thrust as he charged forward, killing many.

Used two handed, the spear has increased reach compared to one-handed use. The com-

Above: When used two-handed, the spear has the advantage of extremely long reach, notably in a lunge, where the shaft can slide so that the butt end is in the outstretched hands. Left: Atli observed that "broad spears are in fashion, now," after being run through by Þorbjörn. (*Bas relief: Halldór Pétursson*)

batant no longer needs to hold the spear near its center of balance, but instead, he can bring his hands back towards the butt end of the spear.

In a thrust, the spear shaft can slide so that both hands are at the butt end of the shaft, allowing the spear to reach the full extent of the shaft in a lunge, greatly extending the reach of the thrust.

Two-handed use of the spear also works well in single combat and is described in the sagas. In chapter 45 of *Grettis saga*, Þorbjörn Arnórsson knocked loudly on the door at Bjarg, the farm of Atli Ásmundarson, then he hid behind the house. When Atli went to the door, Þorbjörn rushed up holding his spear in two hands and

ran Atli through. "Broad spears are in fashion, now," Atli observed, and he fell dead.

A spearhead found near Dalvík in north Iceland is 36.5 cm (14 in) long and 5.4 cm (2 in) wide, broader than is typical for Viking-age spears. Perhaps Þorbjörn's spearhead looked something like this example, and Atli thought its shape worthy of comment after being run through with it.

When used two handed, the spear provides the combatant with enough leverage to lift his opponent up off his feet, impaled on the tip of spear. Þórólfr Skalla-Grímsson did just that with Earl Hringr in chapter 53 of *Egils saga*.

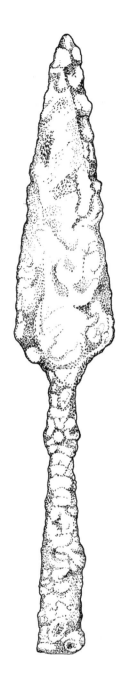

Perhaps Þorbjörn's spearhead resembled this Viking-age spearhead found near Dalvík in west Iceland. (*Illustration: Michéle Hayeur-Smith, Fornleifastofnun Íslands*)

I once thought that the spear, despite its advantage of reach, was slow, compared to a weapon like the sword. I have been shown otherwise. A spearman can keep a swordsman very busy, flicking the point from face to belly and back again, while staying out of range of the sword. However, a spearman would need to be wary that anyone armed with a sword didn't find his way past the point of the spear. Once past the point, the swordsman would have every advantage. The stories say that fighters armed with swords had the ability to cut spear shafts in two with their swords, rendering the spears nearly useless. For instance, in chapter 31 of *Finnboga saga ramma*, as Jökull Ingimundarson thrust at Þorkell Sigurðarson with a spear, Finnbogi Ásbjarnarson cut the spear shaft in two with his sword.

One approach that seems to work well when a swordsman faces a spearman is for the swordsman to adopt the inside guard with his shield, inviting an attack.

When the spearman thrusts, the swordsman can move to outside guard, deflecting the thrust.

The swordsman steps in behind the shield and places himself in a perfect position to lop off the head of the spear. From here, the swordsman is well situated to control the shaft of the spear with his shield as he closes the distance to attack the spearman.

The spearman, now holding a stick, still has many good options; the fight is not yet over. For example, he could step out, choke up, and use the butt end of the spear against the swordsman. The spearman might have avoided having his spearhead lopped off in the first place by shortening his grip, bringing his spear under the shield, and attacking the other side.

One response to a spear thrust is to jump over it. In chapter 146 of *Brennu-Njáls saga*, Kári Sölmundarson jumped up as Lambi Sigurðarson lunged at him with a spear. Kári landed on the spear shaft, breaking it.

This sequence illustrates the need for a spearman to be wary of a swordsman. Above: The swordsman on the right adopts an inside guard with his shield, inviting an attack Middle: As the spearman thrusts, the swordsman changes from inside to outside guard, blocking the attack. Below: With a single step, the swordsman is past the point of the spear, and he can simply lop off the head from the spear.

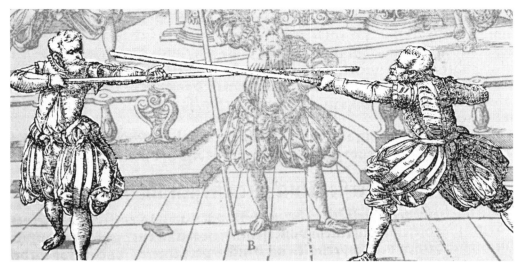

Some of the techniques for staff weapons from the medieval combat manuals, such as Meyer, can be adapted to Viking-age spear, but we do not know if any of these techniques were used in the Viking age. (*Higgins Armory Museum*)

Spears were occasionally used in other ways in combat. In chapter 16 of *Reykdæla saga og Víga-Skútu*, Steingrímr Örnólfsson and his men were battling Áskell Eyvindarson and his men, who were positioned on a bank above a frozen river. Steingrímr's men approached over the ice, but they were at a severe disadvantage because the ice was not sound. Helgi þorbjarnarson vaulted over the weak ice using his spear shaft and up onto the bank where Áskell and his men were fighting. It didn't do Helgi much good because Háls þórisson ran him through immediately, and Helgi fell back dead onto the river ice.

In chapter 6 of *Fóstbrœðra saga*, þorgeirr Hávarsson watched from the top of a snowy ridge as Bultradi laboriously made his way up the slope for a fight with þorgeirr. Bultradi cut steps in the hard, frozen snow with his axe as he worked his way up the hill. Perhaps having grown tired of waiting, þorgeirr set his spear underneath him on the snowy hill, with the spear point facing down the slope, and he slid down the slope on his spear. As he flew by, he drove his axe into Bultradi's chest.

We know little of the details of how spears were used in the Viking age. Some of the later medieval fight manuals teach techniques for staff weapons that can be adapted to Viking-age spears, but as with other weapons, it is not known if those techniques were used in the Viking age.

Talhoffer's manual from 1467 teaches techniques for the messer, a long knife. Similar techniques may have been used with the Viking sax, a short sword.

9

SAXES

A sax is a short sword that was more common-ly used during the early part of the Viking era. It is a short, one-handed, single-edged, knife-like weapon with a blade length ranging from 30 to 60 cm (12 to 24 in).

Saxes usually had simple fittings and no crossguard. Hilts were made of wood, bone, or horn.

Saxes often had a characteristic blade shape with parallel edges, a pointed tip, and a bent or broken, rather than straight, back.

Other blade-shapes are also found, and the distinction between a sax and a single-edged sword is not always a clear one. Some historical sax blades have a gentle curve to the point on both sides of the blade. It is likely that single-edged Viking swords evolved from saxes during the early part of the Viking age. Similar weapons were used in many cultures and in many periods in history. The use of saxes by the Germanic peoples predates the Viking age by centuries, but postdates the Roman era. Tacitus, writing in the 2nd century, said that the Germanic people rarely used swords (*gladius*), preferring javelins instead.

Compared to swords, saxes were typically more crudely fabricated. Rather than being crafted by skilled, specialized smiths, saxes were probably made by local smiths. Blades tended to be heavier and thicker than sword blades. The back edge of a recovered 7th-century sax blade is about 8 mm (0.3 in) thick.

However, not all sax blades were crudely fab-ricated. Some were pattern welded, like sword blades and some spear heads of the period, indicating a higher level of craftsmanship. At least a few sax blades were every bit the equal of the finest sword blades from the period. Additionally, the hilts of some saxes were high-ly decorated with inlay and other techniques.

Saxes were usually carried in a sheath sus-pended horizontally from the belt. A 10th-cen-tury stone cross at St. Andrew's Church in Middleton, Yorkshire, depicts a warrior sur-rounded by his weapons: spear, shield, sword, and axe. His sax is shown suspended from his belt.

The sax was carried with the sharp edge upwards, so that the edge didn't cut through the leather sheath. Thus, the bottom of the sheath had the same broken-back shape as the blade of the sax.

Suspending the sheath with a slight tilt, goes a long way toward preventing the sax from slid-ing out of the sheath accidentally, although there is little to prove that this precaution was taken in the Viking age.

Different length saxes are sometimes referred to by different names, such as *langsax* or *scra-masax*. However, the usual term that appears in

Above: Sax blades ranged in length from 30 to 60 cm (12 to 24 in). This 7th-century sax blade is in the collection of the Higgins Armory Museum. Left: This replica is based on the historical sax shown above. The sheath is based on a find from Trondheim. Above right: The replica blade was fabricated using pattern welding, a process described in more detail in the chapter on swords. The thick, solid backbone of the sax, both in the original and in the replica, is 8 mm (0.3 in) thick. Below right: The sax was a rugged, trusty weapon, equally suited for a fight or for farm chores. This replica sax is based on an 8th-century sax found in the Netherlands.

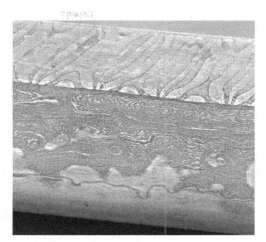

Above left: Saxes usually had simple fittings and no crossguard, although this replica sax hilt is decorated with inlay on some of the hilt components. Above right: Like the original, this replica sax also has an exquisite pattern-welded blade. Right: Saxes were carried in a sheath suspended horizontally from the belt, either in front or on the back. This image from a 10th-century stone cross in England shows a warrior surrounded by his weapons, with his sax suspended in front from his belt.

Suspending the sax sheath with a slight tilt goes a long way toward preventing the sax from sliding out of the sheath accidentally during vigorous movement, but there is little to prove that Vikings took this precaution. The reenactor stands in the front door at Eiríksstaðir, a Viking-age house reconstruction in west Iceland.

the saga literature is *sax* and, rarely, but equivalently, *höggsax* and *handsax*.

Some people preferred a sax over a sword for fighting. In *Grettis saga*, for example, it is said that Grettir Ásmundarson favored his sax, called *Kársnautr* (Kar's Gift), which he took from Kár's grave mound.

One of the more memorable descriptions of the use of a sax in a fight occurs in *Brennu-Njáls saga*, at the fight at the Eystri-Rangá river described in chapter 63. Kolr Egilsson thrust at Kolskeggr Hámundarson with his spear while Kolskeggr had his hands full with other opponents. The spear went through Kolskeggr's thigh. Kolskeggr stepped forward and cut off Kolr's leg with his sax, and he asked, "Did that get you or not?"

Kolr replied that it was what he deserved for not shielding himself. He stood looking at his leg stump.

Kolskeggr said, "You don't need to look, it's just as it appears: the leg is gone." Then Kolr fell down dead. The fight took place near the boulder *Gunnarssteinn* (Gunnar's stone) adjacent to the river.

Information about the use of the sax is scantier than for other Viking weapons. Relatives of the sax, including long knives such as the falchion, the messer, and practice weapons such as the dusack are taught in the later manuals, such as Meyer, Dürer, and Talhoffer. A messer technique from Talhoffer is shown in the illustration facing the chapter title. Some of these techniques are applicable to the Viking sax. However, these manuals do not teach the use of these weapons in combination with a shield. As taught in the manuals, these weapons are used simultaneously for offense and defense, and as a result, many of the techniques are not directly applicable to sax and shield combat.

We have found that many of the sword and shield techniques apply directly to the sax.

The stone Gunnarssteinn marks the site where Gunnarr and his brothers were ambushed adjacent to the Eystri-Rangá river in south Iceland. During the fight, Kolskeggr cut off Kolr's leg with his sax and asked, "Did that get you or not?"

However, the sax, being single edged, does not permit any of the short-edge tricks that make a sword so versatile, as are described later in the chapter on sword and shield techniques.

This 8th-century Viking sword from a private collection typifies early Viking-age swords. (*Photo: Francis G. Morano*)

10

SWORDS

MORE than anything else, the sword was the mark of a warrior in the Viking age. They were difficult to make, and therefore rare and expensive. The author of *Fóstbræðra saga* wrote in chapter 3 that very few men were armed with swords in saga-age Iceland. Of the 100-plus weapons found in Viking-age pagan burials in Iceland, only 16 are swords.

A sword might be the most valuable item that a man owned. The one sword whose value is given in the sagas is the one presented by King Hákon Haraldsson to Höskuldr Kollsson in chapter 13 of *Laxdæla saga*. It was said to be worth a half mark of gold. In saga-age Iceland, that represented the value of sixteen milk cows, a very substantial sum.

Swords were heirlooms. They were given names and passed from father to son for generations. The loss of a sword was a catastrophe. Chapter 30 of *Laxdæla saga* tells the story of Geirmundr gnýr (thunder), who planned to abandon his wife þuríðr Ólafsdóttir and their baby daughter in Iceland. þuríðr boarded Geirmundr's ship in the harbor at night where he slept before his departure. She took away his sword, *Fótbítr* (Leg Biter) and left behind their baby. þuríðr rowed away in her boat, but not before the baby's cries woke Geirmundr. He called across the water to þuríðr, begging her to return with the sword.

He told her, "Take your daughter and whatever money you want."

She asked, "Do you mind the loss of your sword so much?"

"I'd have to lose a fortune before I minded as much the loss of that sword."

"Then you will never have it, since you have treated me dishonorably."

The historical sword shown on the facing page represents a typical sword from the early Viking age in excavated condition.

Swords were typically double edged; both edges of the blade were sharp. Swords were used single handed because the other hand was busy holding the shield. Blades ranged from 60 to 90 cm (24 to 36 in) long, with 70 to 80 cm being the most typical. The widest part of the blade was typically 4.5 to 6.0 cm wide (1.8 to 2.4 in). The hilt and pommel provided the needed weight to balance the blade, with the total weight of the sword a bit more than 1 kg (2.2 lb). An extraordinary 9th-century sword found in Norway is an ungainly 1.9 kg (4.2 lb). Blades had a slight taper, which helped bring the center of balance closer to the grip. In addition, blades had a fuller, a central depression on both faces of the blade created when the blade was forged. The fuller forms an I-beam-like shape that results in a lighter blade without sacrificing stiffness or strength.

Not every historical Viking sword is a gem. As with any group of artisans, it is clear that bladesmiths in the Viking age varied in their level of skill. Historical Viking-age swords I

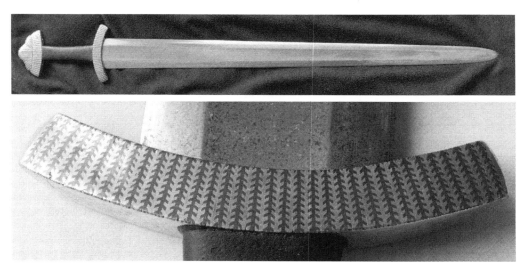

This replica sword is based on a 10th-century sword found in the Thames in London. Above: Like the original, this blade has a greater taper than is typical for Viking swords and also has an elaborate iron inlay. Below: The hilt components were inspired by a 10th-century Norwegian sword with an exquisite herringbone inlay of precious metals, shown in greater detail in a later photograph.

have personally handled run the gamut from magnificent specimens that leap into the hand and become a natural extension of the arm, to pathetic lumps of iron that want only to fall back to earth, opposing the swordsman's will at every opportunity.

The hilt of a Viking sword is made up of the pommel, upper guard, grip, and crossguard. On the historical example shown on the facing page, the organic materials making up the grip have decayed and fallen away in the centuries since this blade was made, revealing the tang, the narrow extension to the blade that passes through the crossguard and grip and fastens to the upper guard. The crossguard has been pulled up from the blade to reveal the shoulder, where the blade narrows to form the tang.

Both edges of the physical blade are nominally identical. However, in describing sword technique, it is useful to distinguish one edge from the other because they are used in different ways.

The later German combat treatises call the two edges of a double-edged sword the *long edge*

and the *short edge*. The long edge (also called the *true edge* in later English combat manuals) is the "front" of the blade, the edge in line with the knuckles. The short edge (*false edge*) is the "back" of the blade. Cuts with the long edge are more powerful, but the later manuals teach the benefits of short-edge attacks, as described in the next chapter.

Which edge of the physical blade is long and which is short depends solely on which way in the hand the sword is being held.

The photo on page 108 shows four historical Viking-era sword hilts, illustrating a few of the variations in crossguards and pommels that existed during the Viking age. The hilts are generally classified using a system devised by Jan Petersen and published in 1919.[7] Because a

7. Jan Petersen. *De Norske Vikingsverd: En Typologisk-Kronologisk Studie over Vikingetidens Vaaben* (Kristiania: Videnskapsselskapets Skrifter II. Hist.Filos. Klasse, 1919).

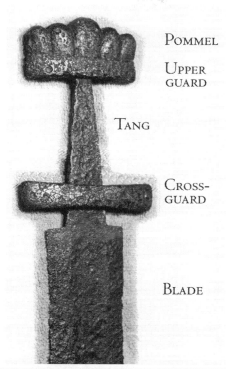

POMMEL

UPPER
GUARD

TANG

CROSS-
GUARD

BLADE

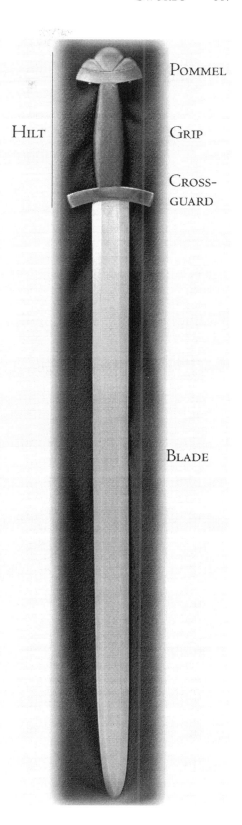

HILT

POMMEL

GRIP

CROSS-
GUARD

BLADE

LONG EDGE

SHORT EDGE

The parts of a Viking-age sword are called out in these three images. The crossguard of the historical sword shown above left has been pulled away from its normal position in order to reveal where the blade narrows to form the tang. The other two swords are modern replicas.

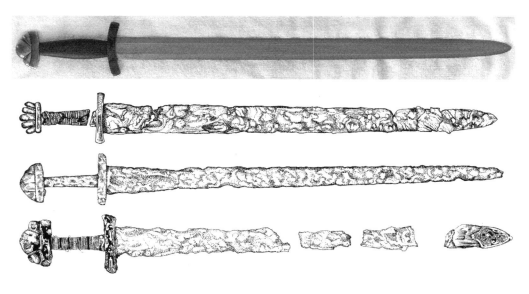

Above: This replica sword is based on a 10th-century sword found in east Iceland. Middle: The shortest of these three Viking-age swords found in Iceland is 91 cm (36 in) overall. (*Illustration: Michéle Hayeur-Smith, Fornleifastofnun Íslands*) Below: These four historical swords show some of the variation in hilt styles used during the Viking age. These variations were classified by Jan Petersen in 1919 and can be used to help date a sword.

given style was in use only during a given period, the hilt style can be used to help date a sword.

Not only did the size and shape of the hilt components vary, but also the construction details. One example of this variation is the way

in which the pommel was fastened to the tang.

In the early part of the Viking period, the tang was peened onto the upper guard, and the pommel was attached to the upper guard. The hilt pictured at the top of page 110 has retained its upper guard but is missing its pommel. In

Left: This Petersen Type B hilt suggests that the sword was made between the middle of the 8th century and the beginning of the 9th. Right: This Type K hilt suggests a date squarely in the 9th century. Both swords are from a private collection. (*Photo: Doug Whitman*)

the later part of the period, the pommel attached directly to the tang.

These sorts of variations can be used to help date a sword.

In cases where the pommel was attached to the upper guard, the pommel was fastened with rivets, adhesives (such as pitch), or other means. The historical pommel shown on the next page has separated from the sword of which it was once a part. However, the fasteners that formerly attached it to the upper guard remain intact.

Hilt components were decorated using several techniques, including scribing and wire inlays.

The inlay was created by cutting myriad tiny channels into the iron of the pommel, and then by fitting and hammering tiny pieces of wire into each of the channels. The work is extremely tedious and time-consuming, but it results in a striking appearance, which can also be seen in the historical sword upon which the reproduction shown on the next page was based.

Stories say that sometimes fighters used their swords two handed. For example, in chapter 10 of *Þorskfirðinga saga*, Már Hallvarðsson fought Askmaðr inn þungi and Kýlan. Askmaðr had bewitched Már's sword so it wouldn't bite. Már

Top: In the earlier part of the Viking era, the tang was peened onto the upper guard (right) and then the pommel was fastened to the upper guard. Later, the pommel attached directly to the tang (left). Middle left: This pommel has been separated from the sword of which it was once a part, but the fasteners that once attached it to the upper guard are intact. Middle right: Hilt components were usually decorated. This historical pommel is decorated with scribed concentric circles. Bottom left: The guard on this historical sword is inlaid with gold. (*Photo: Francis G. Morano*) Bottom right: This replica pommel is inlaid with copper and silver in a herringbone pattern.

Left: The grips of typical Viking-age swords are short, as seen on this replica sword, with just enough room for one hand, but not for two. Right: Some historical grips are so short that one wonders whether the swords were gripped with the smallest finger over the pommel, as illustrated in this 12th-century manuscript. This kind of grip would seem to have significant disadvantages for the swordsman.

threw down his shield and used his sword with two hands, bludgeoning Kýlan's shoulder and breaking his shoulder bone.

THE grips of most surviving Viking-age swords are quite short, with just enough room for one hand, but not for two. It is not clear how a sword with a grip this short could be effectively wielded with two hands.

Some surviving grips are so short that students of Viking-age combat have speculated that the sword was held by three fingers and the thumb, with the smallest finger resting on the pommel. From a martial arts perspective, I find that suggestion very unconvincing. The combatant's hold on his sword would seem to be weakened, resulting in a less secure grip on the weapon, and in poorer balance, in my opinion.

I would be inclined to dismiss the idea out of hand except that some manuscripts from the Viking age have illustrations that show this kind of three-finger grip. Even a 12th-century man-

uscript shows this grip, from a time when swords and their hilts had grown in length making this kind of hold on the sword unnecessary.

I wonder if perhaps the manuscript illustrator used a stylized rendering of the human hand that gives us a false clue today. There are far more examples of period illustrations showing a conventional five-finger grip, including examples in 10th-century Anglo-Saxon manuscripts.

Most historical Viking-age swords have grips large enough for a conventional five-fingered grip. The average hilt length for the collection of Viking swords cataloged by Peirce is 92 mm (a bit more than 3.5 in).[8] Many historical Viking-age swords have grips large enough for even the most ham-fisted Viking to grip comfortably, such as the Icelandic swords shown on page 108. All three have grips longer than 100 mm (4 in). This evidence makes it hard for me to believe that a three-fingered grip was com-

8. Ian Peirce. *Swords of the Viking Age.* (Woodbridge: The Boydell Press, 2002.)

Above: These illustrations from 10th-century Anglo-Saxon manuscripts show a more conventional grip on the sword. Middle left: Grips on Viking-age swords were often wrapped, usually with leather. This historical sword uses a wrapped grip made from highly speculative modern materials. Below left: This replica sword uses a leather wrap on the grip that more closely resembles what probably was used in the Viking age.

mon, and practical consideration of the use of the sword makes it hard for me to believe that such a grip was desirable.

An instance where a combatant might have been forced to use a three-fingered grip was in cases where a sword had been in use for a long time and had been repaired multiple times. In such cases, the hilt would have grown shorter over the life of the sword. Each time the pommel and upper guard were removed from the tang for renewal, it is possible that some small

portion of the tang was lost. Perhaps a combatant using an oft-repaired sword with a short hilt might have found it necessary to adopt this kind of grip.

Sword grips were made from a variety of materials, ranging from a simple wooden grips to elaborately decorated grips wound with wire made from precious metals, or covered with embossed plates of precious metals. Although spectacular in appearance, sword grips made this way would have provided a less secure grip than other materials. Leather-wrapped wood would have provided a better grip, and ivory or bone were probably used because these materials don't get slippery when wet. The archaeological evidence is slight, however, because these organic materials degrade.

Geirmundr gnýr's sword *Fótbítr* (Leg biter) is described in chapter 40 of *Laxdœla saga* as having a hilt made of walrus ivory. Later in the saga, Bolli Bollason owned the sword, and when he returned to Iceland from his service with the Varangian Guard in Constantinople, the hilt was wrapped with gold, as described in chapter 77.

Dᴜʀɪɴɢ the early part of the Viking age, sword blades were made with a process called pattern welding. This technique was used because there was no single material good enough for making sword blades, with the proper combination of strength, flexibility, and ability to hold a sharp edge.

In the past, it was believed that at least part of the difficulty was that the iron-making process was not understood or well controlled during the Viking age. Smiths could not consistently create high-quality steel in their smelting furnaces. They recognized good steel when they accidentally made it and set it aside for special uses, but good steel in quantities sufficient for making sword blades was not available until the later part of the Viking age.

As this text is being written, however, experimental archaeologists are reporting that they obtain consistent, repeatable results with their experimental smelting operations using period techniques and tools. Perhaps Viking-age smiths had much greater control over their smelting process than was previously thought.

To make a usable sword blade with the available materials in the Viking age, the smith created a composite material using the pattern-weld-

Blade fabrication using the pattern welding process began by welding multiple layers of different types of iron into a bar. This welded bar has been ground and etched to reveal the seven layers of iron used in its fabrication. (*Photo: Jeffrey L. Pringle*)

ing technique. He started by stacking together selected bars of different types of iron in a specific order. He used soft, low-carbon iron for flexibility, and hard, high-carbon iron (steel) for strength and edge-holding ability. This bundle of iron bars was welded together into a solid, layered bar.

Next, the welded layered bar was forged out to the correct length, and then into a square cross section with desired dimensions. The actual dimension of the bar at this point depended on how many of these layered bars will be used to make up the finished blade. A typical sword, having two or three layered bars in the core, required a bar about 13 mm square (1/2 in).

The smith heated and twisted the bar of layered iron.

Multiple twisted iron bars were stacked together in preparation for fabricating the blade. In most cases, the bars were squared before stacking to ensure the best possible joins when they were welded together. The dimensions of the individual bars making up the stack ranged from 6 to 16 mm square (1/4 to 5/8 in), depending on how many bars were being stacked to make up the blade. The three inner bars which make up the core of the blade shown on page 115 are about 10 mm square (3/8 in).

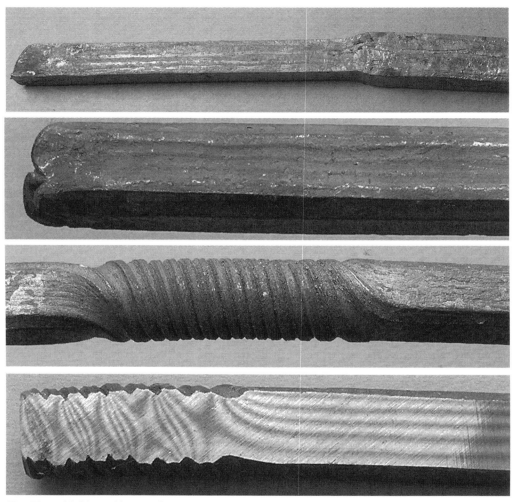

Top: The welded layered bar was forged out to the correct length. Only the left side of this bar has been forged Middle above: The bar was forged to a square cross section. Middle below: The bar was heated and twisted. Bottom: The internal structure of the resulting twisted layered bar has been revealed by grinding and etching the bar. (*Photos: Jeffrey L. Pringle*)

To create a blade capable of holding a sharp edge during use, Viking-age swords typically were fabricated with edges made of steel. The steel that will form the edge was wrapped around the three twisted bars making up the core of the blade.

Most historical blades appear to have been fabricated this way. This approach has the advantage of requiring only a single welding step to form the blade from the layered bars. The stack of bars in the photograph on the next page is now ready to be welded into a solid unit.

In some cases, two separate strips of steel were used for the edge. The grain of the steel reveals whether separate strips were welded on to each edge and joined at the point, or whether a single strip was wrapped around the point.

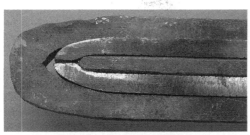

Top: Steel that will form the cutting edge of the sword has been wrapped around the three twisted bars that will form the core of the blade. (*Photo: Jeffrey L. Pringle*) Bottom: The grain visible on a historical sword tip shows that a single strip of steel was wrapped around the tip to form the edges, rather than two separate strips.

A replica blade is assembled and finished in this sequence of photographs. A different replica blade is shown, having four bars in the core, rather than three as in the replica shown to the left. Top: The steel edge is fitted to the core that has already been welded. Middle above: The steel edge has been welded to the core, forming a solid blade. Middle below: The blade has been forged to the correct shape. Bottom: The fuller has been formed, and the edges have been beveled. The rough hammered object is starting to take on the appearance of a smooth, finished blade. (*Photo: James Austen*)

Some historical swords show evidence of two separate welding processes. First, the core of twisted layered bars was welded together, and then the steel edge was welded to the core. Then the blade was forged to the correct shape, widening and thinning the blade.

The fuller was then formed in the center of the faces of the blade, and the edges beveled. Finishing operations take the blade from a rough, hammered object to a smooth, finished object.

The blade was filed to remove surface irregularities left from the hammering and to true up lines and tapers. The file marks were removed with abrasive stones.

Bladesmiths were capable of creating a mirror-like finish in the Viking age, and some modern bladesmiths have suggested that blades were finished to this degree. A highly-polished blade with its finer surface would have resisted corrosion better than a less finished surface.

The complicated and demanding pattern-welding process resulted in the creation of a composite material. Alone, none of the individual types of iron used in the process had the required properties for a sword blade, but the composite that resulted did have the necessary strength, flexibility, and edge-holding ability for a robust and trusty blade.

Above: The replica blade is finished. The exquisite pattern in the blade has been brought out by polishing and etching, probably to a greater degree than would have been common in the Viking age. (*Photo: James Austen*)
Left: This historical pattern-welded blade has steel edges and three twisted bars in the core.

Despite the use of this complex fabrication technique, the stories say that swords occasionally failed at critical times. During an extended battle, swords sometimes became so dull that they no longer cut. In chapter 109 of *Óláfs saga Tryggvasonar*, King Óláfr asked his men why they cut so slackly (*slæliga*) at the Battle of Svölðr because he could see that the blades did not bite. His men replied that their blades had become too dull and dented to cut.

The sagas give examples of swords that were broken in battle, such as in chapter 30 of *Heiðarvíga saga*. Eiríkr viðsjá (the cautious) delivered a powerful cut to Þorljótr Þorbjarnarson, and the sword blade broke in two. Eiríkr picked up the broken end of the blade and struck again, killing Þorljótr.

The stories also describe instances in which a sword blade bent during a fight. In chapter 49 of *Laxdæla saga*, Kjartan Óláfsson was ambushed as he rode up Svínadalur valley. He was not carrying his usual sword, a gift from King Hákon Haraldsson to Kjartan's grandfather, but rather a lesser sword. Several times during the battle, the blade bent under the force of the blows.

Kjartan had to straighten his bent blade by standing on it to continue the fight.

In addition to creating a blade with more suitable physical characteristics, the pattern-welding process creates a blade having a stunning, exquisite appearance. The process forms beautiful, delicate patterns in the surface of the blade as the different types of iron come to the surface.

Bladesmiths often combined the twisted layered bars in artistic arrangements. Layered bars twisted in one direction were placed next to layered bars twisted in the opposite direction. Twisted patterns were alternated with linear patterns. The reproduction sword blade shown above illustrates both of these techniques in use.

One sometimes wonders how much of the twisting was done for decorative purposes and how much to control the material's properties.

Later in the Viking era, pattern welding was no longer needed because the iron-making process became better controlled, resulting in the availability of larger quantities of better iron. Smelting operations created good, homogenous steel with the required properties for a

The pattern welding process creates beautiful, delicate patterns in the surface of the blade. Top left: This replica pattern-welded blade has not been etched, and the patterns on its surface are extremely subtle. Top right: The linear pattern on the left of this historical blade changes to a twisted pattern on the right. (*Photo: Francis G. Morano*) Middle: This replica sax, like the original on which it was based, has an exquisite pattern-welded blade. Left: This detail of the replica sax blade shows extremely fine patterns in the body of the blade and coarser patterns in the strong backbone.

sword blade. It is also possible that high-quality crucible steel from the Middle East and Asia came into the hands of some Viking-era bladesmiths, such as those located along the Rhine. Regardless, pattern welding continued to be used until near the end of the Viking age, for decorative purposes, and as a mark of quality.

BECAUSE very few sword blades survive from the Viking age with even a trace of their original finish, we can only speculate on the appearance of the surface of Viking sword blades when they were new. The blades shown on this and the following page represent what is believed to be a very good guess.

One of the few surviving examples of a historical blade from the Viking age with its original finish is shown on the following page. Although it was cleaned after excavation, it likely retains much of its appearance from when it was new. This blade also has an inlay, one of several decorative techniques applied to blades in the Viking age. Blades were sometimes inlaid with metals such as iron, silver, or gold. In some cases, the inlays were simply decorative.

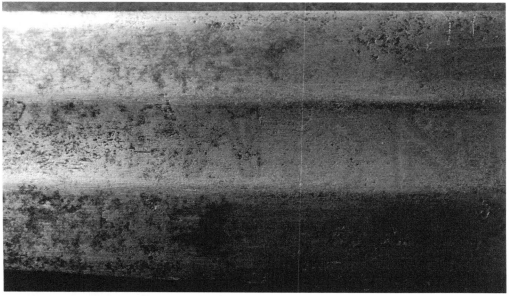

Above: This excavated 11th-century sword in a private collection survives in excellent condition. It is possible that Viking-age blades looked something like this when new. The blade is not pattern welded, but rather is made from a monosteel, a single type of steel. The blade also has an iron inlay. Left: Like the historical blade, this replica blade is also made from a monosteel. The replica was polished using techniques and materials known to have been used in the Viking-age, so it is possible that new blades in the Viking age had a similar finish.

Decorative inlays were often geometric designs, including roundels, bars, and crosses, but some were pictorial, depicting, for example, wolves, snakes, and birds. Phrases, such as "in nomine domini" (in the name of the Lord) are found. In other cases, the inlays are the maker's name or mark.

Two common maker's marks are *Ingelrii* and *Ulfberht*. The Ulfberht mark often appears with crosses on either side of or within the name, as shown on the facing page, and usually with geometric inlays on the reverse side of the blade. So many swords with the Ulfberht mark survive,

manufactured over such a long period of time that they cannot possibly be the work of one smith. More likely, the swords are the product of a workshop where generation after generation of bladesmiths worked. The shop is thought to have been located in the middle Rhine region, in Frankish lands.

Iron inlays were created by chiseling grooves into the blade to form the letters or symbols. Pattern-welded iron was drawn into wire, then fitted and hammered into place in the grooves. Finally, the blade was heated to forge weld the wire into place. The inlays typically were placed

Top: The Ulfberht mark often appears with crosses on either side of or within the name, as seen in this historical blade. Bottom: Inlays are rare in pattern-welded blades, although this pattern-welded Viking-age blade from a private collection has an inlay.

entirely within the fuller of the blade, although there are examples where the inlay extends outside of the fuller.

Inlays are rare in pattern-welded blades, although some do exist. Inlays are far more common in monosteel blades.

In chapter 5 of *Fljótsdæla saga*, Þorvaldr Þiðrandason, while in a troll's cave, found a sword with a green colored blade without a spot of rust, a description suggesting the blade was made of bronze. I am not aware of any archaeological evidence for the use of bronze blades in the Viking age, although a bronze axe head was found in a Viking-age context in Iceland.

Most of the Viking-age swords in the Norse lands appear to have come from the Frankish lands in continental Europe, in what is now Germany. Archaeological evidence suggests that

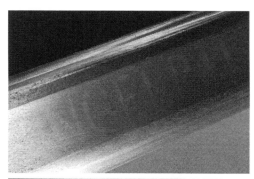

Above: The iron inlay in a modern replica blade is very subtle in normal lighting. Below: The inlay is much more visible in this replica, which was etched to bring out the appearance of the inlay. The pattern welding of the wire inlay is highly visible. (*Photo: Jeffrey L. Pringle*)

some swords arrived as unfinished blades in Viking lands, where they were finished and fitted with hilts locally. It also seems likely that specialized smiths in Viking lands developed the skills needed to fabricate sword blades, but evidence to support the conjecture is weak.

There are a few instances in the sagas in which people are described fabricating weapons, but never swords. One example is in chapter 23 of *Fóstbræðra saga*, in which Bjarni made a special axe for Þormóðr Bersason.

The stories suggest that some swords were acquired as gifts: from kings, from earls, or from family members. Weapons were taken from grave mounds by men brave enough to enter the grave and battle the ghostly mound-dweller.

It is not clear how men maintained their weapons. The stories are filled with examples in which, during hard use, a weapon became so dull that it no longer cut. Sharpening weapons must have been a routine chore, as it was with agricultural implements. In many cases, men sharpened their own weapons, but in a few cases, they asked others to do the job for them.

In chapter 9 of *Droplaugarsona saga*, Helgi Droplaugarson asked Þorbjörn, a servant at the farm at Eyvindará to sharpen his sword. The saga says that Þorbjörn was good at sharpening weapons. Helgi left his sword with Þorbjörn, who lent him another sword to use while his was being serviced.

There also appear to have been professional sword sharpeners. In the battle at the Alþing described in chapter 145 of *Brennu-Njáls saga*, it is said that after Skapti Þóroddsson was wounded by a spear, he was dragged into the booth of a sword sharpener to protect him from the ongoing battle.

Prior to a battle, men prepared their weapons. There is a description of Njáll's sons preparing for a battle in chapter 44 of *Brennu-Njáls saga*. Skarpheðinn sharpened his axe, Grímr attached his spearhead to a shaft, Helgi riveted the hilt of his sword, and Höskuldr fixed the handle on his shield.

Archaeological evidence shows that weapons were sometimes repaired after they suffered damage. Several surviving historical swords have blades that were broken in two and then welded back together and returned to use.

The sagas confirm that swords could break during a battle, such as in chapter 1 of *Gísla saga*. Kolr, a slave, asked Gísli Þorkelsson to return the sword *Grásíða* that Kolr had lent him. Gísli refused, and so Kolr attacked him. Gísli struck Kolr's skull with *Grásíða* using such a powerful blow that the blade broke.

Top left: Broken swords were often repaired or repurposed. Þorgrímr forged the broken sword Grásíða into a spear at his forge in the Haukadalur valley in west Iceland, shown as it appears today. Top right: Swords were heirlooms passed from generation to generation. Ásdís gave her son Grettir the sword owned by her grandfather. (*Bas-relief: Halldór Pétursson*) Below: Swords were refitted as needed and used for centuries. At some point during this sword's working life, an 11th-century crossguard was fitted to a pre-Viking-age blade made centuries earlier.

The stories also give examples of broken weapons that were repurposed and forged into other weapons.

Later, in chapter 11 of *Gísla saga*, Þorgrímr nef and Þorkell Súrsson took the broken pieces of Grásíða and made them into a spearhead that measured one handspan in length. Þorgrímr's forge was located in the Haukadalur Valley.

Swords were highly prized heirlooms during the Viking era and were used for generations. When a young man, Grettir Ásmundarson pre-

pared to leave Iceland to travel to Norway, as told in chapter 17 of *Grettis saga*. His father, Ásmundr Þorgrímsson, had a low opinion of Grettir and refused to give him a sword, saying, "I don't know what useful work you would do with weapons." His mother, Ásdís Bárðardóttir, who was more supportive, gave Grettir the sword owned by her grandfather Jökull Ingimundarson.

Archaeological evidence also supports the long and continued use of sword blades. One

Left: The scabbard that protected this early Viking-age sword rotted away, leaving traces of the wood from the scabbard adhering to the blade. Right: Near the point of the same blade, fiber-like structures are visible on the blade, thought to be the remains of the fleece that lined the scabbard. The sword is from a private collection.

sword was found with an 11th-century cross-guard fitted to a blade made during the migration era, centuries before the Viking age.

This evidence suggests that sword blades several centuries old continued to be maintained and used.

A sword's scabbard provided protection for the blade when not in use. Because scabbards were made almost entirely from organic materials, few Viking-age scabbards have survived. What does survive tends to be bits of organic materials from the scabbard stuck to the blade and the hilt components. Thus, our knowledge of Viking-age scabbards is sparse.

Scabbards were probably made as a sandwich, with multiple layers to protect the sword blade. The outermost layer was leather, which covered and protected the scabbard. It's possible that linen was used in place of leather on some scabbards. The next layer was wood, which provided the physical strength and structure of the scabbard. There is evidence that some scabbards had yet another layer, made of fleece or wool located between the wood and the blade. The natural oils in the wool would have helped protect the blade from rust.

Many scabbards had metal chapes at the tip, to protect the point of the scabbard and sword, and some had metal mounts at the throat of the scabbard.

A sword without a scabbard was considered "troublesome" (*vandræða*), as in difficult to manage. In chapter 6 of *Hallfreðar saga*, King Óláfr Tryggvason gave Hallfreðr vandræðaskáld (troublesome poet) a sword without a scabbard, a troublesome gift for a troublesome poet. The king said that Hallfreðr must keep it for three days and three nights without harm coming to anyone.

Above: Chapes covered and protected the tip of the scabbard. This bronze chape was found at Lundur in north Iceland and is about 5.7 cm (2 in) long. (*Illustration: Michéle Hayeur-Smith, Fornleifastofnun Íslands*) Right: Early in the Viking age, swords were slung from a baldric, a belt over the shoulder, as modeled by this re-enactor. Later, swords were more typically slung from a waist belt.

In chapter 39 of *Harðar saga*, Þorbjörg Grímkelsdóttir wanted to get her husband's sword away from him so she could give it to an assassin she had secretly hired. She intentionally damaged the scabbard so that the sword fell out on its own. Rather than taking a sword without a scabbard, Þorbjörg's husband Indriði Þorvaldsson took no sword when he left to settle a dispute among his friends.

There are examples in the sagas where swords stuck fast in their scabbards. In one case, the sword had supernatural properties and was being abused, as told in chapter 9 of *Kormáks saga*. The sword finally came out of the scabbard howling. In *Hrólfs saga kraka*, a legendary saga with many fantasy elements, Böðvarr Bjarnarson's sword was stuck fast in the scab-

bard when he tried to draw it against a troll, as is told in chapter 23. Böðvarr worried the sword back and forth fiercely until he could slide it out of its scabbard. It makes one wonder how often this sort of thing happened in actual combat.

Early in the period, scabbards were usually slung from a *baldric*, a belt over the shoulder. Later, swords hung directly from the waist belt.

The stories say that some swords had a looped strap (*hönk*) on the hilt which could be pulled over the hand, allowing the drawn sword to hang while another weapon was being used.

In chapter 57 of *Egils saga*, Egill Skalla-Grímsson drew his sword and pulled the loop over his hand in preparation for a fight with Berg-Önundr Þorgeirsson. During the fight, when Egill's *kesja* (an unknown pole weapon

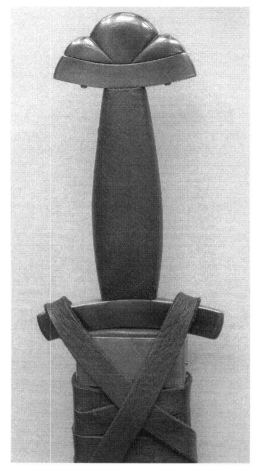

Above: The sagas talk about a hönk, a looped strap on the sword hilt that allowed the sword to hang from the wrist while using another weapon. A speculative reconstruction is shown using replica weapons. Right: This replica scabbard has peace-straps (friðbönd), which prevented the sword from being drawn in anger in places where weapons use was prohibited.

usually translated as *halberd*) stuck fast in Berg-Önundr's shield, Egill grabbed his sword and was able to run Berg-Önundr through before his opponent could even draw his sword.

We don't know the nature of the loop on the hilt of Egill's sword. Surprisingly, though, when hung from the wrist, the sword did not seem to be much in the way when executing some typical actions with the spear during a practice session. None of its motions caused any concern that a sharp edge might bite unintentionally. One would certainly want to be cautious about crossing one's hands, though, to make sure the sword hand always crossed below the other hand. After the pole weapon was dropped, a simple flick of the wrist brought the sword up into the hand.

The stories talk about the use of a peace strap (*friðbönd*), straps to prevent the sword from being drawn in anger in places where its use was prohibited.

An example of the use of a friðbönd occurs in chapter 28 of *Gísla saga*, at the *várþing* (spring assembly) that took place at þorskafjarðarþing in west Iceland.

Bergr and Helgi, the two young sons of Vésteinn, arrived at the þing unrecognized. Approaching þorkell Súrsson, they complimented him and asked to see his fine sword. þorkell agreed and handed over the sword in its scabbard. Bergr undid the peace straps and drew

Booth ruins remain visible at Þorskafjarðarþing in west Iceland today. At the þing meeting one spring, the young boy Bergr undid the peace straps on Þorkell's sword and used the weapon to lop off Þorkell's head, avenging his father's death at Þorkell's hands.

the sword. Þorkell said, "I didn't give you per-mission to draw the sword." The boy responded, "I didn't ask," and lopped off Þorkell's head, avenging the death of his father by Þorkell.

It is not known how weapons were used in the Viking age. Our research suggests a sophisticated combat system was employed, using subtle tricks against an opponent to gain an advantage.

11

VIKING-AGE SWORD AND SHIELD COMBAT TECHNIQUES

As described in earlier chapters, it is not known how weapons were used in the Viking age. The Vikings left little behind that teaches us their techniques. The best we can do is to make some educated guesses based on later combat treatises and other sources.

A disclaimer: These materials are for reference and study purposes only. Historical combat is potentially dangerous. Students wishing to explore these techniques should do so only under the supervision of a qualified, experienced teacher of historical martial arts.

There are some who would believe that in the Viking age, fights took the form of two hairy men trading great blows with one another, almost as if they were trying to chop down trees.

Our research suggests that instead a sophisticated system of martial arts was in use during the Viking age. Men used a variety of subtle tricks to cause their opponents to shift their defense, creating an opening that could be exploited. Men used all parts of their weapons to gain the advantage over their opponents.

We believe that Viking-age fights took the form of brief, intense exchanges of attacks and counterattacks, followed by a withdrawal out of range to regroup and to plan the next attack. Each combatant began in a ward or guard (a starting position) and selected an attack meant to get past the opponent's defenses. Fighting

men did not simply enter a fight and flail away at their opponents willy-nilly. Men entered a fight with a plan: with a set of attacks in mind suitable for the weapons in use and for the opponent that they faced.

The medieval German combat treatises talk about the three parts to an exchange: the onset (*Zufechten*), which is the initial attack from a distance; the handwork (*Handarbeit*), which is the action after the swords have engaged; and the withdrawal (*Abzug*), which is the attempt to disengage without being struck. Each exchange was an attempt to degrade the opponent's level of control by means of a series of quick attacks.

The later treatises teach the value of attacking first to one quarter of the opponent and then to another quarter. Meyer's treatise of 1570 shows how a man should be divided into quarters and suggests drills for developing skill in attacking to alternate quarters. Each attack draws the opponent's defenses to a new quarter. Ideally, the attacker shifts his attack and targets another quarter even before contacting his opponent's defense.

Any one of these attacks could hit its target and end the fight, but a skilled opponent could be expected to parry the attacks. The repeated attacks to alternating quarters, however, reduces the opponent's ability to defend, making it less and less likely he can parry each subsequent

Meyer's combat treatise of 1570 shows how an opponent should be divided into quarters and teaches that a combatant should attack to alternating quarters. (*Higgins Armory Museum*)

attack. Thus, the combination of attacks has a better opportunity to cause the opponent to make a mistake, allowing an attack to get past the opponent's defenses.

A goal of the combatant is the attrition of his opponent. The combination of attacks wears down the opponent, not only physically, but also mentally. The opponent's coordination, concentration, and control are reduced.

There is an analogy in the modern game of tennis. During a volley, the player in control would prefer to return the ball first to one side of the opponent's court, then to the opposite side, forcing the opponent to have to run the width of the court between returns, wearing him down. A skilled player could be expected to return the ball the first time or the second time, but his ability to return the ball is degraded by his constant running from one side of the court to the other.

The same holds true in Viking combat. A series of attacks, first to one target, then to another, wears down the opponent, degrading his ability to respond appropriately, and eventually creating an opening that can be exploited.

A corollary to this approach is that a combatant must always keep the initiative to remain in control of the series of attacks. Thus, a fighter strives to be the first to attack and, failing that, strives to regain the initiative during an exchange of blows. A fighter defends with a technique that is also a counterattack. During an exchange, a fighter withdraws if, after a small number of attacks, a blow has not landed on the opponent, lest the fighter's own ability to control the attacks should start to degrade.

Another aspect of the shape of combat is the very aggressive use of the shield. Although it can be used as a passive defense, it is much more effective when used very actively.

Last, there are some fundamentals that might not be obvious to the layman. For example, the combatant must maintain a stance that allows good balance and ease of movement. Stepping out from an incoming blow is an excellent defense, while stepping around to bring a target within range is an important part of offense. The grip on the sword must be fluid, neither too tight nor too loose, so the sword can move in the hand as needed.

Most martial arts systems have a series of *wards* or *guards*: positions that one adopts in which the combatant has good offensive and defensive options, and which also give him a chance to size up an opponent and decide what to do next.

Combatants begin in relaxed stances with the shields nearly parallel to the line of engagement, the imaginary line that connects the two opponents. This position gives a combatant a clear view of the opponent, with the shield in an

It is not known if Vikings used guards when they fought. A reenactor illustrates some possible guards, adapted and named from the medieval German combat treatises. Top left: High guard threatens a powerful attack. Top right: Ox guard is a considered to be a versatile guard in the combat treatises. Bottom left: Change guard hides the sword behind the shield where the opponent can't easily see it. Bottom right: Plow guard is well suited for thrusting.

aggressive, forward position (see illustration facing the chapter title).

This position puts the forward edge of the shield well away from the combatant's body, where it can deflect or otherwise spoil an incoming attack well before it reaches its target.

Some guards that may have been used by Vikings (adapted and named here from the German longsword tradition) include:

High guard, with the sword held high. This guard not only threatens but also telegraphs a powerful downward attack.

Ox guard with the sword held alongside the head like the horn of the ox and aimed at the opponent's face. The later manuals suggest that this is a very versatile guard.

Plow guard with the sword point aimed at the opponent's face or belly and well suited for a thrust.

Change guard with the sword held alongside the combatant's leg, hidden behind his shield and body. The opponent has a hard time seeing the sword in this guard.

EARLY German longsword manuals teach a different version of the high guard, often called *Day,* with the sword held closer to the shoulder. It is not clear if this form has an advantage over the later form of the high guard when applied to sword and shield.

The shield can be placed in the *outside* shield guard or in the *inside* shield guard. When the inside shield guard has been adopted, the sword arm must pass over the shield arm for the higher sword guards and under it for the lower guards.

Guards represent positions that not only permit a variety of attacks but also offer a defense against likely attacks. A guard that does not offer a good defense is unwise, such as the example shown on the facing page. It allows a strong attack. It invites the opponent to attack, which can be useful in some circumstances. However, it does not permit an effective defense. There is no strong defense against the opponent's obvious response of coming in under the blade to grapple.

In the German longsword tradition, a guard represents the beginning or the end of a technique, such as a cut or a wind. A *wind* is a technique taught in the later combat treatises in which a combatant rotates his blade around his opponent's blade to get past the opponent's defense for a follow-up attack. In winding, for example, the combatant moves from the ox guard on one side to the ox guard on the other side when the sword is held high. These techniques begin and end in guard positions having good defenses and having a range of offensive options. The manuals teach that a combatant should not linger in any one guard, but that he

Opposite Left: Earlier European combat manuals, such as Ringeck's treatise from around 1450, teach an alternate version of the high guard, with the sword near the shoulder. Opposite Right: For most of the guards, the shield can be placed outside (to the left for a right-handed man) as shown in the earlier photos, or to the inside as shown here. Guards represent positions that permit a variety of attacks but also offer a good defense. Left: A reenactor demonstrates a poor guard, one that does not permit an effective defense.

should instead seize the initiative before his opponent has time to analyze his options.

There is not, to my knowledge, anything in the sources that suggests which guards were used by Vikings, or even that Vikings used guards at all in their combat. However, given the importance of guards not only in a wide variety of later medieval combat manuals, but also in many other forms of martial arts from other historical periods, it seems probable that skilled Viking-age fighters were familiar with and used guards.

A variety of cuts and thrusts were probably employed. The range of cuts used by Vikings probably included a high cut coming straight down from above, meant to split the skull in two; a high diagonal cut, which attempts to separate neck from shoulders; a horizontal cut, which can target anywhere from neck to thigh; and a low rising cut, which attacks anywhere from the leg up to the armpit.

Attacks can be made from either side. It might at first seem that the shield is in the way of a cut from the left. An image in Talhoffer's combat treatise of 1467 illustrates the use of

longsword and dueling shield, which are both much larger than Viking-age weapons. Both of the combatants have swept their shields from the outside to the inside and are thrusting over their shield arms.

A similar approach seems to work quite well with Viking-age sword and shield. Attacks can be made above and below the shield arm when the shield is on the inside.

Evidence suggests that sword and shield combat targeted every part of the body. Forensic evidence from Viking-age skeletal remains shows evidence of wounds from head to lower leg. When targets are mentioned in the sagas, the head, upper body, and legs are all mentioned with nearly equal frequency, whereas arms and back and shoulders are mentioned less frequently.

Even the names of weapons tell us something about common targets. Bolli Þorleiksson's sword in *Laxdæla saga* was named *Fótbítr* (Leg Biter), which suggests that the leg was considered a fine target for a sword attack in the Viking age.

This conclusion contradicts the teachings of the later combat manuals, and it represents a

Top: Using Viking sword and shield, attacks can be made from either side, attacking over or under the shield arm as necessary. Talhoffer's manual from 1467 shows both combatants thrusting over their shield arms. Bottom: The medieval combat manuals teach that leg cuts should be avoided because a leg cut can easily be trumped by a scalp cut. The combatant on the right has delivered a cut targeting the leg. His opponent on the left has stepped backwards, removing the target, and is delivering a scalp cut to the head. The combatant on the right is about to receive a painful lesson on the folly of an attack to the leg with the longsword. This advice does not apply to Viking sword and shield combat, where the shield can be used independently to block the scalp cut.

good example of a situation where the later manuals cannot be applied to Viking sword and shield fighting.

The later manuals teach against using leg cuts. With a weapon like a longsword, a leg cut can easily be trumped by stepping backwards and delivering a cut to the head, a technique called a scalp cut. The geometry favors the scalp cut.

With sword and shield, the combatant holds offense in one hand and defense in the other, and as a result, the dynamics differ from those of longsword combat. A leg cut can't easily be trumped by the scalp cut because the shield defends against a cut to the head as the leg cut connects. Forensic evidence, saga evidence, and common sense suggest that the leg is a good target when using sword and shield, against the advice of the later masters teaching different weapons.

In a fight, it does no good to attack the opponent's shield. Behind his shield, an opponent is well protected. Instead, one must attack the opponent's body. As a result, a primary objective of an attack is to fake or trick the opponent into moving his shield, drawing it out of the way, and opening up a new target for a subsequent attack. One can imagine tricks in which a blow is targeted at one quarter, causing the opponent to move his shield to defend. That response gives the attacker the opening he needs. He can pull his blow or otherwise deceive his opponent and retarget the blow at the available opening.

Similar techniques show up in the later treatises. One of the key tactics in the German longsword tradition is to deliver an attack to one quarter, drawing the opponent to defend there, and then to pull away to deliver a subsequent attack to another quarter, as described earlier. We have applied this approach to Viking-age sword and shield and find it is equally effective with those weapons.

The ox guard for longsword and dueling shield is illustrated in Talhoffer's 1467 treatise.

For example, the later medieval combat treatises teach that the ox guard is a particularly useful and versatile guard for a variety of weapons, as illustrated in Talhoffer's 1467 treatise. From this position, a combatant can target a cut or thrust to the face or head and then, when the opponent repositions his shield, pull the attack and strike to the lower quarter. Did fighting men in Viking times use this guard or use these tricks? We don't know. The photo sequence on the next page shows a modern interpretation of a sequence using this trick.

This elementary sequence illustrates the concept of attacking to one quarter to draw away the opponent's defense, then pulling the attack to target the resulting opening in another quarter. A skilled combatant, however, is unlikely to be as unresponsive as **B** (the combatant on the left) was in this sequence. A trained, experienced fighter might expect **A**'s attack and be prepared to respond in an appropriate matter.

ATTACKING TO ALTERNATE QUARTERS. Top: **A** (the combatant on the right) begins in ox guard, and **B** (the combatant on the left) begins in plow guard. Bottom: **A** delivers a thrust to **B**'s face, who responds by bringing his shield up to defend. The sequence concludes, opposite above, with **A** pulling his thrust, and cutting to **B**'s unprotected leg

As a result, the two combatants are likely to continue their handwork (their attacks and counterattacks), until either an attack lands on its target, or until the two combatants withdraw into a guard to prepare to fight again.

Let's extend the sequence, a step at a time, to illustrate this concept. Each new sequence begins using the identical moves as the previous sequence. However, in each case, the combatant who took the blow that ended the previous

sequence reacts using a response consistent with the principles of the later combat manuals and blocks the attack while delivering a blow to his opponent to end the sequence. The final sequence ends with a withdrawal, in which the combatants separate, retreating into a guard to begin the fight again.

These sequences do not appear in any of the later combat manuals and are based solely on conjecture. However, we believe that the techniques illustrated here follow the principles laid out in the later manuals.

We start with the sequence of moves illustrated on this and the facing pages. In the subsequent photographs, the two combatants will have reversed positions to make their moves more clearly visible.

A CUTS TO B's LEG

RECAP: **A** (on the right, opposite) begins in ox guard, with his shield in outside guard. **B** (on the left) begins in a plow guard, with his shield in outside guard. **A** thrusts to **B's** head. **B** raises his shield to defend. **A** pulls the thrust and cuts to the opening on **B's** exposed leg.

COMMENTARY: This technique shows up repeatedly in the later manuals. A combatant delivers an attack to one quarter. As the opponent shifts his defenses to that quarter, the combatant pulls and attacks to the opening provided by his opponent.

B CUTS TO A's HEAD

RECAP: **A** and **B** begin as above. Turning to the photo sequence on page 136, **A** (now on the left) thrusts to **B's** head and then pulls the attack to cut low.

RESPONSE: As the thrust comes in, **B** steps out with his right foot and steps back on his left foot, removing **A's** target. **B** delivers a short edge cut to **A's** head.

COMMENTARY: **B** recognizes the feint and removes the obvious target. Then **B** attacks to the opening. **B** might choose to attack to the head from a higher angle than is shown in the photo. This is very effective, and it allows **B** to deliver either a cut to the head or neck, or a devastating thrust to the face.

A CUTS TO B's ARM

RECAP: Continuing the action on page 137, **A**

thrusts and then pulls the attack to cut low. **B** steps out and back to cut to **A**'s head.

RESPONSE: When **A** senses his target moving away, he brings his shield up and back to block **B**'s short-edge attack to the head and simultaneously brings his sword up in front of him for an attack to the other side. **A** cuts to **B**'s exposed arm (opposite, top).

COMMENTARY: **A**, realizing that his target has vanished, retargets his attack. **A** moves his shield to block **B**'s attack, a move which also conveniently positions **B**'s arm for the attack.

B Applies a Shield Bind to A

RECAP: **A** thrusts and pulls the attack to cut low (top). **B** steps out and back to cut to **A**'s head (bottom). **A** brings his sword up to attack to **B**'s arm (opposite, top).

RESPONSE: As **A** raises his right arm for the attack, **B** steps around and aggressively binds **A**'s

An extension of the previous sequence. A and B reverse sides for better visibility. Opposite top: In a recap of the previous sequence, A (now on the left) delivers a fake thrust to B's head, followed by a cut to B's leg. Opposite bottom: B, recognizing the feint, steps out and back, removing the target. B delivers a short edge cut to A's head. Above: A, sensing his target has vanished, brings his shield and sword up. A blocks the head cut with his shield and slices to B's exposed arm. Below: As A raises his sword arm to attack, B aggressively binds A's sword arm with his shield and cuts to A's leg.

sword arm with his shield, preventing **A** from making his attack. **B** cuts to the inside of **A**'s leg. COMMENTARY: **A**'s attack to **B**'s arm is an obvious choice. As **A**'s sword goes up, a quick thinking **B** might recognize a good opportunity to apply a shield bind to **A**'s raised arm. Additionally, **B** is well set up for a thrust under his shield to **A**'s belly, an attack that **A** can't easily see.

A WITHDRAWS

RECAP: **A** thrusts and pulls the attack to cut low. **B** steps out and back to cut to **A**'s head (page 136). **A** brings his sword up to attack **B**'s arm.

Opposite top: The extended sequence concludes. To avoid **B**'s shield bind and end this exchange, **A** brings his shield between himself and **B**'s shield, and he aggressively shoves **B** away with his shield. **A** withdraws into a guard. Opposite bottom: A SEQUENCE ILLUSTRATING A SHIELD BIND. **A** (now on the right) adopts the plow guard while **B** (on the left) adopts a high guard. Above: **B** delivers a powerful high cut to **A**'s head.

B steps out and begins to apply a shield bind (page 137).

RESPONSE: To avoid the shield bind and to end this exchange, **A** steps into **B** before the bind is applied. **A** swings his shield between his body and **B**'s shield, opposite top. Using his shield, **A** shoves **B** away, and the two combatants retreat into their guards. **A** and **B** prepare for another exchange.

COMMENTARY: The later combat manuals teach that a combatant should limit an exchange to only a few maneuvers before retreating into a guard lest his ability to control the attacks start to degrade. **A** avoids the shield bind by shoving **B**, then he withdraws into a guard.

We believe this kind of short, intense exchange was typical of Viking-age combat. When executed at speed, this full sequence of five attacks and counterattacks takes fewer than two seconds, yet any of the attacks could have been lethal if the other combatant had not been prepared with a ready response.

In this sequence, **B** used a shield bind on **A**, a powerful technique. The next sequence, beginning with the bottom illustration opposite, highlights the effectiveness of a shield bind at opening new lines of attack and immobilizing an opponent.

A SHIELD BIND

A (opposite, below, on the right) begins in plow,

The sequence concludes. Top: **A** simultaneously drops the point of his sword, steps out from under the attack, and sweeps his shield to the inside, across the space between the two combatants. This move catches **B**'s incoming attack and forces it off line. Bottom: **A** has bound **B**'s sword and now controls both of **B**'s weapons, as well as **B**'s body. **A** can bring his point back on-line for a thrust to **B**'s exposed side.

shield outside. **B** (left) begins in high, shield outside.

B delivers a high cut to **A**'s head. As the cut comes in, **A** drops the point of his sword, steps off line to the side, and sweeps his shield from outside to inside, catching **B**'s incoming attack and forcing it off line, as shown opposite, top. The later manuals teach again and again the benefits of an attack to the head. The sagas say that attacks to the head could have lethal results, despite the protection of a helmet. Therefore, **A**'s response most likely would have been trained, rather than a natural reaction.

A brings his point back on line and thrusts to **B**'s exposed side. **A** has completely bound up **B** and controls his sword, his shield, and his body, shown opposite, below. A thrust to the side is quick, but slices to the exposed back or legs would also work.

This shield bind seems effectively to end the fight. Once in a shield bind, a combatant has few options. Although not apparent in the photos, **A** has excellent control, not only over **B**'s weapons, but also over **B**'s body. **B**'s weapons are useless, and **A** has good targets at the head, shoulders, back, and legs. There is no more work that **B** can do except to die.

This sequence is an excellent example of a situation in which the shield is used to control the opponent's weapon, not through contact with his weapon, but rather through contact with his body.

We have found the shield bind to have surprisingly wide applicability in all phases of a fight: in the onset, as part of the first contact between combatants; in the handwork, when combatants are engaged; and in the withdrawal, as combatants separate.

The technique of the shield bind shares some similarities with *Verkehren* (Reversing), a technique described in later longsword treatises such as Meyer and Ringeck. Meyer describes revers-

ing as a way to trap your opponent while giving yourself space to work at will, which is exactly the effect of applying a shield bind. All of our sword and shield interpretation is based on speculation, but it is reassuring when similar techniques show up in later treatises. Such instances lend support to our conjectures.

THE shield bind is such a powerful technique for ending a fight that we wondered if there might be some way to avoid it. Although not mentioned in the later manuals, one conjecture that appears promising is for **B** to decline the shield bind.

Declining a Shield Bind

RECAP: **B** and **A** begin as before. **B** attempts to deliver a high cut, and **A** steps out and begins to sweep his shield to catch **B**'s incoming attack.

RESPONSE: However, **B**'s attack is a fake. **B** executes a *running off* to the outside, and he does not step forward with his fake cut, page 142, top. Running off is a deceiving technique taught in the later manuals in which the sword is rotated around the hilt. The hilt stays in place while the blade continues to move, causing **A** to believe the attack continues, when in fact, **B** is gathering for an attack elsewhere. **A** continues to execute the shield bind. **A**, meeting no resistance, overshoots, allowing **B** to attack to the head or to another target, page 142, bottom.

COMMENTARY: **B** has other alternatives here for declining the bind. Whatever he chooses, he must convince **A** that the attack continues, so that **A** overcommits to the shield bind.

IF a combatant can't trick the opponent into creating an opening, he may have to create his own opening. One example is shown in the illustration from Talhoffer's treatise shown on

A SEQUENCE IN WHICH THE SHIELD BIND IS DECLINED. Top: **A** and **B** begin as before. **B** (on the left) prepares to deliver a high cut to **A**'s head. As the attack comes in, **A** steps out to deliver the shield bind as before. **B**'s attack is a fake. **B** executes a running off to the outside. Bottom: **A** is completely taken in by the fake. Meeting no resistance, his shield bind overshoots, allowing **B** a clear attack to the head or other opening.

this page. The combatant on the left has just kicked his opponent's shield from outside to inside guard, creating an opening for a thrust.

A modern interpretation of this trick using Viking sword and shield is shown in the photos on the following three pages.

Creating an Opening with a Kick

A (on the left) begins in change guard, shield outside. B begins in plow, shield outside (page 144, top).

A makes a low rising short edge cut to B's legs, under B's shield, while stepping forward. B brings his shield down to defend. This puts B's shield in a good position for A to turn his step into a kick (page 144, bottom).

A kicks B's shield to the inside and brings his sword up for an attack to the opening. B is thoroughly bound up by the momentum of A's kick. A is free to cut to the neck, shoulders, back, or legs as he pleases (page 145, top).

Showy tricks like this are not without their hazards. A's unprotected leg is a very inviting target for B, or for another combatant nearby.

Declining the Kick

A and B begin as above. A cuts to B's legs, but B steps back as A attacks. A, already committed to the kick, meets no resistance and overshoots (page 145, bottom).

A's exposed leg makes for an inviting target, although an attack to head or neck could also work here (page 146, top).

As a result of this encounter, A is likely to earn a new nickname that is occasionally mentioned in the sagas: *tréfótr* (wooden leg).

The later medieval combat treatises teach the advantages of closing the distance to grapple during a fight. There are instances where a combatant might step right in to his opponent, converting the sword fight into a wrestling match,

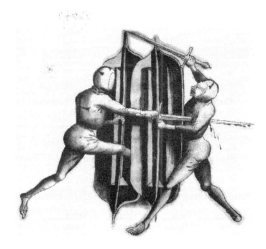

If an opponent will not move his shield to create an opening, a combatant may simply have to do the job himself. Talhoffer's treatise of 1467 teaches one such technique.

and pinning his opponent's arms and weapons or executing a disarm or a throw.

From the sagas, we know that Vikings enjoyed wrestling and practiced it as a sport. At the Hegranessþing spring assembly in north Iceland, young men thought it would be good to arrange wrestling matches, as told in chapter 72 of *Grettis saga*.

Grettir Ásmundarson, who was an outlaw at the time, was unrecognized, and he was urged to participate in the contests because he appeared to be a strong contender.

Did Vikings also practice wrestling in combat? The Viking-age swords were short enough that, when two combatants were in sword range, it was only a short step to be within grappling range, so it seems quite possible.

There are several examples in the Icelandic sagas where grappling is described as a normal part of combat. In some cases, an unarmed man grappled with an armed man who attacked him, as is told in chapter 19 of *Bjarnar saga Hítdœlakappa*. As Björn Hítdœlakappi walked out of the farmyard with his visitor Þorsteinn

A SEQUENCE ILLUSTRATING HOW TO CREATE AN OPENING WITH A KICK. Top: **A** (on the left) begins in charge guard. **B** (on the right) begins in plow. Bottom: **A** makes a low rising cut while stepping forward. **B** lowers his shield to defend.

The sequence concludes. Top: As **A** steps forward to make his cut, he kicks **B**'s lowered shield from the outside to the inside, simultaneously shifting his low attack to the neck, back, or any convenient opening. A SEQUENCE IN WHICH THE SHIELD KICK IS DECLINED. Bottom: As before, but as **A** attacks, **B** steps back, removing the obvious target. **A**, already committed to the kick, overshoots.

The sequence concludes. A's exposed leg makes an inviting target for **B** or for one of his friends fighting nearby, but an attack to A's head or neck would also work.

Kálfsson, he realized that Þorsteinn had come as an assassin. Björn, who was unarmed, moved away, giving Þorsteinn an opening. Þorsteinn raised his axe to strike, but Björn went under the axe to grapple. Björn threw Þorsteinn down, then strangled him.

In other cases, an armed man might choose to discard weapons that had become useless, and close the distance to grapple. In chapter 65 of *Egils saga*, Egill Skalla-Grímsson's and Atli Þorgeirsson's shields had both become useless from the exchange of blows during a duel, and the combatants threw them away. Egill also threw away his sword and grappled with Atli, eventually killing him by biting through his throat.

Hávarðar saga Ísfirðings tells of a situation in chapter 21 in which the sword of Atli inn litli (the small) wouldn't bite. He threw away his sword and went underneath Þorgrímr Dýrason's defense to grapple with him.

I once thought that grappling would be difficult with Viking-era shields. Talhoffer, however, describes a grappling technique with dueling shield and mace which works well with Viking sword and shield.

The sequence of photos on the next two pages shows a modern interpretation of Talhoffer's technique applied to Viking-age weapons.

A GRAPPLE AND A THROW

B (page 148, top, on the right) delivers a high cut to **A**.

A discards his sword and shield. He brings his right arm up to block and deflect **B**'s incoming blow.

A grabs **B**'s hand to control **B**'s weapon and pulls forward to throw **B** off balance, while stepping forward in front of **B**.

A reaches behind **B**'s neck with his left arm and throws **B** over his hip.

Above: The combat treatises teach that there are times when a combatant should drop his weapons and grapple. Talhoffer's treatise of 1467 teaches a grappling technique for mace and dueling shield that seems to apply to Viking sword and shield. Right: Vikings enjoyed wrestling as a sport. Grettir arrived at the þing at Hegranes and was invited to participate in the wrestling matches taking place at the assembly. Today, booth remains are still visible at the site. Grettir's island hideaway of Drangey is visible in the distance.

The importance of grappling in the later manuals, the ease with which Talhoffer's technique can be applied to Viking shields, and the presence of wrestling as a sport in Viking society suggests that Vikings were familiar with and utilized grappling techniques in their combat.

Additionally, this sequence serves as an example of how the later medieval martial arts treatises are only a memory aid, rather than a textbook. Talhoffer provides few details in his description of the action. The photographs are an extremely simple interpretation of the action taught by Talhoffer.

A combatant showing more skill than **B** would likely find a way to escape from **A**'s control, as the technique is executed here. Similarly, a combatant showing more skill than **A** would want to control **B** and **B**'s weapon more securely, as well as wanting to cast **B** down in a manner that makes it more likely that **B** would suffer injuries in the fall.

LATER combat treatises, such as Meyer's, describe three phases for each exchange in a fight: onset, handwork, and withdrawal.

A GRAPPLING TECHNIQUE FROM TALHOFFER ADOPTED TO VIKING SWORD AND SHIELD. Opposite top: **B** (on the right) delivers a high cut to **A**. Opposite bottom: **A** discards his sword and shield. He brings his right arm up to block and deflect **B**'s attack. Top, above: **A** grabs **B**'s arm to control his weapon and pulls forward to throw **B** off balance. **A** steps in front of **B**. Bottom: **A** reaches behind **B**'s neck and throws **B** over his hip.

Fights could go on for such a long time that men grew weary and rested. At the fight at Eyvindarstaðir in east Iceland, shown as it appears today, Þorvarðr grew tired and rested against a wall. The episode suggests that Viking-age fighters had effective withdrawal techniques that allowed them to disengage without being struck.

Talhoffer's techniques for longsword and dueling shield focus on the onset. Little is said about handwork and nothing about withdrawal. So how do two combatants fighting with Viking sword and shield withdraw? We are finding few satisfactory answers.

The shield seems to make useless the withdrawal techniques that are taught in the later manuals, which teach that during withdrawal, a combatant seeks to disengage without being struck by his opponent. Typically, a combatant delivers a cut to cover his retreat. The cut has little chance of connecting, but it does serve to discourage his opponent from following as the combatant retreats.

However, when fighting with Viking-age sword and shield, the shield removes much of the threat from these out-of-range attacks. The shield can block these attacks, allowing the opponent to step in and follow with further blade work as a combatant attempts to retreat. Egill Skalla-Grímsson did just that during his duel with Ljótr inn bleiki (the pale), described

in chapter 64 of *Egils saga*. Every time Ljótr yielded ground, Egill followed him, staying on him, and striking furiously.

We know from stories in the sagas, such as the fight at Eyvindarstaðir described in chapter 18 of *Vopnfirðinga saga*, that earnest fights could go on for a very long time without any wounds being inflicted. Þorvarðr grew so weary during the fight that he threw himself down against a wall to rest while the fight continued around him.

Chapter 172 of *Íslendinga saga*, a contemporary saga, says that a fight continued well into the night, and at times, men rested as if playing in a ball game.

These sorts of passages strongly suggest that an effective withdrawal technique existed for sword and shield combat. One technique that shows promise is to initiate a withdrawal with a shove. When two fighters are bound up with little additional work that either can do, a combatant can shove forward and then step backwards. Doing so opens the space between them, allowing the combatant to judge available options, and either to withdraw safely or to prepare a new attack.

The photo opposite shows an interpretation of the shove. **B** (on the right) is attempting to apply a shield bind, while **A** (on the left) initiates a withdrawal by shoving and then stepping away.

To the opponent, the shove is confusing because it is not immediately clear whether the shove is initiating continuing pressure leading to an advance, or is an attack meant to cause the loss of balance, or whether it is merely a jerk that provides the time and space for a withdrawal.

Fights could go on for such a long time that combatants might ask for a truce, or for a break in the fight to recover their strength. In chapter 9 of *Gunnars saga Keldugnúpsfífls*, Gunnar Keldugnúpsfífl rode out to Örn's farm, knocked

A shove can be used to initiate a withdrawal when fighting with sword and shield. The combatant on the left shoves his opponent away, opening a space for safe withdrawal.

on the door, and told Örn to defend himself. They fought for a long time. Örn tired before Gunnar, because he was an older man, and he asked Gunnar for a pause. They rested, leaning against their weapons. When they began the fight again, Örn fought with renewed vigor, but Gunnar eventually cut through Örn's helmet and skull, killing him.

A truce during a fight was sacrosanct. It was abhorrent and shameful to break a truce, although the stories say that it occasionally happened. One truce breaker was Hrafn Önundarson, described in chapter 12 of *Gunnlaugs saga ormstungu*. Gunnlaugr ormstunga and Hrafn fought for a very long time. Eventually, Gunnlaugr hacked off Hrafn's leg. Hrafn dropped back onto a tree stump, and the two men discussed the fight. Hrafn asked for a drink of water, and Gunnlaugr asked for and received

promises that Hrafn would not trick or deceive him. Gunnlaugr brought water in his helmet to Hrafn. As Gunnlaugr handed over the helmet, Hrafn struck a powerful blow to Gunnlaugr's head with his sword. Gunnlaugr killed Hrafn, but Gunnlaugr eventually died from his head wound. To repay Hrafn's family for their kinsman's cowardly betrayal, Gunnlaugr's father, Illugi inn svarti (the black), mutilated and killed a number of Hrafn's relatives.

Viking shields are large enough to temporarily blind an opponent to an incoming attack, a trick that may be used to advantage. An incompetent combatant can also temporarily blind himself with his own shield if he's not careful, blocking his own view of his opponent's attack.

Talhoffer teaches the value of swapping sword and shield from one hand to the other, which confuses the opponent and allows attacks

Talhoffer's manual of 1467 teaches the value of swapping sword and shield from one hand to the other during a fight, as the combatant on the right has just done.

to unguarded quarters. In the illustration above, the combatant on the right has shifted his sword to his left hand and makes a thrust to his unprotected opponent.

The sagas say that this technique was used in the Viking era as well. In chapter 10 of *Droplaugarsona saga*, it is said that Helgi Droplaugarson showed his skill in arms in a fight against Hjarrandi. Helgi threw up his sword and shield and caught them in the opposite hands, which allowed him to strike a blow against Hjarrandi's thigh.

We have found that the technique, exactly as described in the saga, works very well. It is extremely confusing to the opponent because the swap appears at first to be merely a change in guard.

Later medieval combat treatises teach the value of cuts made with the short edge (back edge) of the sword. Several of the master cuts, considered to be essential for effective combat in the German longsword tradition, are short-edge cuts. An illustration of the short-edge *Schielhauw* (squinter cut) with a longsword is shown opposite above, taken from Meyer's combat treatise published in 1570.

Cuts made with the long edge are more powerful, but short-edge attacks have some benefits of their own.

For example, if a combatant delivers a long-edge high cut and his opponent parries with his shield, the combatant is done; there is no more work he can do (page 154, top).

However, if the combatant uses the short edge, and the cut is parried, there is still more

The medieval German combat treatises teach the importance of attacks made with the short edge of the sword. Meyer's manual illustrates the Schielhauw (squinter cut). (*Higgins Armory Museum*)

work that he can do. The attack is less powerful, but the angle of the blade permits additional targets to be reached using the short edge (page 154, bottom).

The high short-edge attack shown in the Meyer manual is likely to be difficult to execute with sword and shield. Most short-edge attacks, however, can be easily turned into a more threatening thrust.

In the example shown on page 155, the combatant on the left, taking advantage of the better angulation of the blade around the shield, has turned his short-edge cut into a thrust to the face.

Another use of the short edge is to deliver a slice around an opponent's defense to his back side, using the increased angulation provided by a short-edge attack to reach behind an oppo-

nent. Viking-age skeletal remains with battle injuries show evidence of this kind of short-edge cut.

The femur (thigh bone) from a Viking-age man shown on page 156 has the clear mark of a sword cut on the surface of the bone. As with many of the blade injuries to the femur in Viking-age skeletal remains, this cut is on the posterolateral shaft: on the outside of the leg to the rear.

A cut to that target is difficult with the long edge but rather easy and straightforward with the short edge. The increased angulation of the blade allows a combatant to reach behind his opponent with his sword to deliver a cut to the rear of the leg.

Opposite top: If an opponent (on the right) parries a long edge attack with his shield, the combatant (on the left) has no more work he can do. Opposite bottom: If, however, the combatant uses a short edge attack, the angulation of the blade allows him to reach around the shield to continue his attack. Above: Further, these kinds of short edge attacks can easily be converted to a more deadly thrust.

This forensic evidence doesn't prove that Vikings used the short edge while fighting, but it is highly suggestive of its use, and apparently with enough power to cut through the leg muscles and into the bone.

Some medieval European combat systems do not make much use of the short edge. Notably, the earliest surviving European combat manual, the *Royal Armouries MS I.33*, does not distinguish the long edge from the short edge in the text. Although the illustrations are not always clear, it appears that virtually all of the attacks are with the long edge.

This example serves to again illustrate how the treatises are memory aids, rather than instructional manuals. The illustration from *I.33* shown on page 157 has been interpreted by some modern students as a short-edge squinter cut to the head from above. The illustration could also be interpreted as a long-edge attack from below. The text gives no indication and merely says, "Beware the head!"

The lack of short-edge attacks in the *I.33* manuscript is not compelling evidence that they weren't used with Viking weapons, nor even that they weren't used in the sword and buckler system taught in *I.33*. The treatise is a highly distilled memory aid that happens to make no specific mention of the short edge.

An additional argument for the use of the short edge is that if you are not going to use the second edge in a fight, why have it? A single-

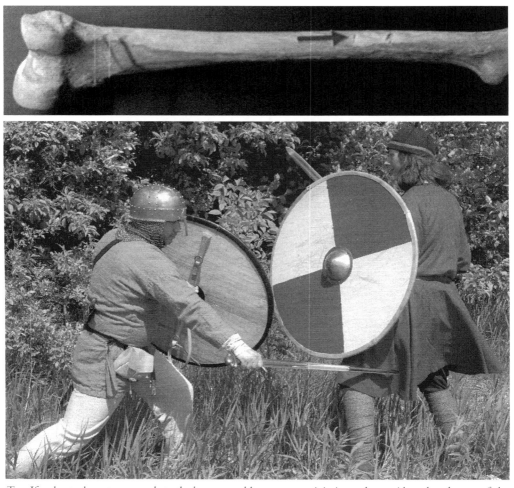

Top: If a short edge cut were made to the leg, we would expect to see injuries to the outside and to the rear of the left leg. That is exactly where most of injuries are found in the leg bones of Viking-age skeletal remains. This 11th-century femur shows evidence of a cut made by a sword in that location. Bottom: It's difficult to reach the back of the leg with the long edge, but the increased angulation of the blade makes it easy with the short edge.

edged weapon, with a strong backbone in place of the second edge, is a much more rugged weapon.

The reproduction single-edged sax and double-edged sword shown in the photos opposite have similar width, but the sax has a strong backbone, apparent in the edge photo, making it a rugged, trusty weapon.

However, the sax lacks the ability to do any of the short-edge attacks that makes the sword such a versatile weapon.

Did Vikings use the short edge in their fights? Given the importance of short-edge attacks in later medieval combat, and the apparent value when applied to Viking sword and shield, and the available forensic evidence, it seems quite possible that short-edge attacks were used by Vikings.

Top: Some medieval European combat systems do not appear to use the short edge at all, such as Royal Armouries I.33. The text doesn't mention its use, although this illustration from the treatise has been interpreted by some students as a short edge attack. Bottom left: A replica single-edged sax and double-edged sword are compared. Both have similar blade widths. Bottom right: The sax has a thick backbone, making it a more rugged weapon than the sword. Why put a second edge on a sword unless you intend to use it?

THE later longsword treatises teach that portions of the sword other than the blade can be used offensively. The pommel, crossguard, and hilt can be used for wrenching, thrusting, catching, and striking, as taught in Mair, Ringeck, Meyer, Starhemberg, and other later treatises.

Most of these tricks don't work well with a Viking-age sword, due to the great differences between the weapons from the different periods,

as a side-by-side comparison of a Viking sword and a 16th-century practice longsword makes clear. The greater lengths of the longsword's grip and crossguard allow it to be used for many more tricks and with greater leverage.

One trick that does work well with Viking sword is to snag the edge of an opponent's shield with the pommel, leveraging the shield out of position.

Left: The pommel may be used for hooking tricks, such as snagging the edge of the opponent's shield. Right: The medieval European combat treatises teach many other tricks for the pommel and crossguard, but most of these tricks are not applicable to Viking-age swords because of the significant differences in the weapons. A replica Viking-age sword (left) is compared to a replica 16th-century practice longsword (right).

In the photos on the facing page, **B** (on the left) has just hooked **A**'s shield with his pommel and pulled it away from **A**'s body. The leverage is significant, and **A** can do little to resist.

Whether **A** resists or not, the same motion **B** used to pull the shield away also sets **B**'s sword point in **A**'s face for a fast and unpleasant follow-up attack.

The sagas say that occasionally the pommel was used to strike a blow. Typically, the blows were not meant to be lethal but rather were intended to humiliate. In chapter 10 of *Hænsa-þóris saga*, þorkell trefill (scarf) told a farmhand to do his bidding, or else he'd plant his sword pommel in the man's nose.

When men were at the Alþing discussing the compensation to be imposed for the slayings in the battle on the heath, as told in chapter 37 of *Heiðarvíga saga*, Barði told Tindr, "I struck you with the hilt because you didn't seem worthy of anything more."

In chapter 82 of *Grettis saga*, Grettir Ásmundarson and his brother Illugi Ásmundarson were living on the island of Drangey, safe from any attack from their nemesis, þorbjörn

öngull (hook). One night, when Illugi was tending his injured brother, their servant Glaumr fell asleep while on guard, forgetting to take up the ladder to the top of the island that kept them safe from attack.

þorbjörn and his men found the ladder down, and they easily climbed to the top of the otherwise impregnable island. They came upon Glaumr, fast asleep. þorbjörn woke Glaumr with a pommel strike to the ear, saying, "Any man who entrusts his life to your care is in a poor position."

The use of the pommel is an example of a technique where the historical sources have little to say, yet some of the combat systems with a living tradition, such as those from Asia, have much to say. In the sagas, strikes with the pommel are rare or nonexistent in earnest combat. The later combat treatises teach hooking, striking, and snagging tricks. Some of the continuously practiced combat systems, however, teach brutally effective techniques with the pommel. Were Vikings aware of these tricks with the pommel? Did they use them? Or, as the sagas might seem to imply, were these pommel strikes

A SEQUENCE DEMONSTRATING HOOKING THE SHIELD. Top: **B** (on the left) has snagged the rim of **A**'s shield with his pommel and begins to pull the shield away. Bottom: In a single motion, **B** pulls the shield away and plants the point of his sword in **A**'s face for a quick and unpleasant follow-up attack.

At Grettir's island hideaway of Drangey in north Iceland, shown as it appears today, Þorbjörn began his attack by waking up the hapless Glaumr with a blow from his pommel.

thought to be unworthy for use against an honorable opponent in an earnest fight? As can be seen in some of the photos and illustrations in the previous chapter, the pommels of Viking-age swords came in a variety of shapes, some of which would seem to make the more brutal uses of the pommel even more effective. Are these shapes merely decorative, or were they designed to facilitate some of these pommel attacks? With the information currently available, we cannot say.

The concept of humiliating an opponent either as a part of, or as a prelude to a fight, is taught in some of the later combat manuals. Lecküchner teaches techniques for the *Messer* (a long knife related to the Viking sax) specifically designed to humiliate the opponent. In one case, the combatant is taught to drop his opponent to the ground and then to sit on him in a such a way that the opponent can not move. The master teaches that in that position, you can eat, drink, or play backgammon while sitting on him. Another technique is taught in which the opponent is disarmed and stuffed into a sack. Although not explicitly stated, the implication is that the humiliation be made complete by then dropping him into a pile of manure.

In the Viking era, when honor was prized above all else, it was considered worse to receive a blow meant to dishonor than to have received a bloody wound. Blows meant to dishonor included attacks with portions of weapons not intended to be lethal, such as the pommel of a sword, or the hammer of an axe; attacks with items that were not weapons; and attacks on parts of the body that were not normal targets, such as the buttocks.

Björn járnhauss (iron skull), a fearsome, overbearing bully of a berserk, arrived at a house where Glúmr Eyjólfsson was a guest, as told in chapter 6 of *Víga-Glúms saga*. When Björn turned his attentions on Glúmr, Glúmr jumped up from the bench, snatched off the bully's helmet, and beat him about the back and head with a log from the fire, which made Björn stumble and fall to the floor. Glúmr kept up the attack until the "hero" ran out the door, thoroughly humiliating him.

In chapter 28 of *Grettis saga*, Grettir Ásmundarson arrived at Auðunn Ásgeirsson's farm to repay him for humiliating treatment during an earlier ball game. Grettir waited inside the dim longhouse, and as Auðunn carried in skin sacks filled with *skyr* (sour curds) to the storeroom in the house, Grettir tripped him. Auðunn fell onto one of the skyr sacks, and the tie which closed the neck of the sack came unfastened. Auðunn leapt up angrily and asked what trickster was there in the house. Grettir identified himself and challenged Auðunn to a fight, but Auðunn said that first, he had to see to the food. He picked up the skyr sack and flung it at Grettir. Skyr flew out of the open neck, covering Grettir with skyr and soiling his clothing. Grettir considered it to be a greater insult than if Auðunn had given him a bloody wound.

To repay Sigmundr Lambason for having composed scandalous verses about their father, the sons of Njáll attacked him, as told in chapter 45 of *Brennu-Njáls saga*. Skarpheðinn drove his axe through Sigmundr's shoulder and pulled forward, dropping Sigmundr to his knees. Sigmundr jumped up, but Skarpheðinn taunted him, "You've just bowed down to me, and you'll fall on mother earth before we part." With two more blows from Skarpheðinn's axe, Sigmundr was dead.

The later combat treatises emphasize the importance of stepping out—stepping to one side or another of the imaginary line that connects the two combatants. When a combatant begins an attack, the opponent is advised to step away from the incoming attack. When delivering an attack, the combatant is advised to step around to open up the target. Meyer says that with correct stepping, you can steal away the ground from your opponent.

The sagas provide some confirmation of the use this technique in the Viking age. One example is in chapter 145 of *Brennu-Njáls saga*. Bjarni Brodd-Helgason cut at Kári Sölmundarson's leg with his sword. Kári avoided the cut by pulling back and turning on his heel, moving to the side of the incoming attack. Later in the encounter, Kári thrust at Bjarni with his spear, and Bjarni fell sideways to avoid the spear.

A natural consequence of stepping to the side is that the two combatants tend to circle one another as they fight.

Many of these fundamentals of combat come together in a short description of a fight in chapter 17 of *Brennu-Njáls saga*. Þjóstólfr arrived at Hrútr Herjólfsson's farm in the night and knocked on the door, then he went around to the back of the house. Hrútr put on tunic and shoes and grabbed his sword to answer the knock. He found Þjóstólfr behind the house and drew his sword. The saga says that Þjóstólfr did not want to be the second to strike a blow. He seized the initiative, as taught by later manuals, and swung his axe at Hrútr. Hrútr stepped away from the attack, presumably to the side to get out from under the incoming blow and to open up a target to attack, as taught by the later manuals. Hrútr deflected the incoming blow with his left hand and took the initiative back by swinging at Þjóstólfr's leg with his sword, cutting nearly through it above the knee. Hrútr rushed at Þjóstólfr, grappled with him, and brought him down. Then, Hrútr struck the death blow to Þjóstólfr's head.

It is not clear how boys trained to learn the use of weapons, or when they started their training. There can be no doubt that boys were trained. The ability to use weapons was a part of everyday life in the Viking age. Boys learned the use of weapons in the same way that they learned the use of other everyday tools, such as carpentry and blacksmithing tools. Weapons use was a life skill, no different from sharpening a scythe and cutting hay, or riding a horse, or building a house.

A boy was likely taught these skills by the grown men in his family, notably by his father, his brothers, and his mother's brothers, all of whom had responsibility for a growing boy in Viking society.

Top: Viking-age boys were taught combat skills by the men of the family, in the same way they were taught other skills they would need in their lives. It is thought that young boys started using wooden swords as soon as they could stand and grasp. Bottom: These 10th-century child-sized iron weapons were found in a child's grave in Norway and are a part of a private collection.

Perhaps they started their training using wooden swords. A few wooden swords and fragments from the Viking age have been found, some of which represent faithful copies of real weapons, but it's not known whether they were toys or serious practice weapons.

It has been suggested that as soon as boys were able to stand and grasp objects, wooden toy swords were put in their hands. Perhaps the first steps in teaching the use of weapons began with boys as young as three years old.

Archaeological evidence suggests that even young boys had exposure to and skill with weapons. A number of child-size iron weapons have been found in children's graves.

The historical sword and axehead shown on this page were found in a child's grave in Norway, along with a similarly sized spear and shield boss.

The sword, probably cut down from a full-sized sword, is only 39 cm (15 in) long. The hilt suggests a date in the first half of the 10th century.

Similarly, a child-size axe was found in the grave of a 10-year-old boy at Straumur in Iceland. The axe head is 5 cm (2 in) long. We don't know if these were training weapons, or weapons meant for use in earnest combat by children, or simply tokens of the family's wealth.

The evidence from the sagas is contradictory. One episode suggests that even older children were not capable of wielding adult-size weapons. In chapter 11 of *Fljótsdæla saga*, Helgi and Grímr Droplaugarson, aged 12 and 10 years, left their home one night to kill þorgrímr tordýfill (dung beetle) for his slander. The boys carried their usual thonged spears (*snærisspjót*),

After the fight at Kársstaðir in west Iceland, shown as it appears today, the twelve-year-old boy Þóroddr was found to have been seriously wounded by Steinþórr. Snorri, the boy's father, immediately gathered men to chase after Steinþórr to repay him for his shameful deed.

but they did not carry their late father's sword because neither had the strength to carry it.

There are other examples that suggest that boys were "excused" from combat. They were not expected to participate, and they were shielded from it. In chapter 8 of *Hrafnkels saga*, Hrafnkell Freysgoði and his men attacked Eyvindr Bjarnason and his party. The boy traveling with Eyvindr did not participate because he didn't think he was strong enough. After the fight began, he was free to ride away on his horse.

In chapter 44 of *Eyrbyggja saga*, the story of the fight in the hayfield at Kárssatðir is told. After Snorri goði broke up the fight, he allowed Steinþórr Þorláksson and his men to ride away without being pursued.

Subsequently, it was discovered that Snorri's 12-year-old son, Þóroddr, had been seriously wounded by Steinþórr. Snorri immediately gathered his men to chase after Steinþórr to repay him for the shameful act of attacking a child.

Other episodes in the sagas suggest that boys did participate in killings, particularly for revenge. There is the example of Helgi Droplaugarson and Grímr Droplaugarson described above, in which the boys killed Þorgrímr tordýfill. Another example is related in chapter 14 of *Hávarðar saga Ísfirðings*. Þorsteinn Þorbjarnarson and Grímr Þorbjarnarson, 12 and 10 years old, attacked and killed the powerful Hólmgöngu-Ljótr (the dueler) to avenge the harsh treatment the boys' father had received at Ljótr's hands.

Even very young boys used weapons to kill, notably in chapter 40 of *Egils saga*.

Young Egill Skalla-Grímsson used an axe to kill a player on the opposing team in a ball game in retaliation for some rough treatment in a game played at Hvítarvellir.

Egill was 6 years old. His mother was pleased and said that he had the makings of a fine viking.

In chapter 42 of *Vatnsdæla saga*, Þorgrímr Hallormsson, the father of the 12-year-old boy Þorkell krafla (scratcher), made a deal with his illegitimate son. If the boy were to bury an axe in the head of Þorkell silfri (silver), one of

Top: Not at all Viking-age men were skillful with weapons. At Hólmr in west Iceland, shown as it appears today, Björn grappled with and disarmed two assassins sent to kill him. Björn bound the men's arms behind their backs, slipped their axes under their bonds, and sent them home in shame. Bottom: Even young children used weapons to kill. After some rough treatment in a ball game played here at Hvítárvellir, young Egill drove an axe through the head of an opposing player. Egill was six years old.

Þorgrímr's rivals, the boy could keep the axe, and Þorgrímr would acknowledge the boy as his son. The boy kept his side of the bargain, and after the killing, he said that it was not too much work to acquire the axe.

The stories suggest that Norse people were familiar with the concept of "mock" combat, called *skylming*. It's not clear whether this "fencing" was sport or practice, or perhaps both. In chapter 12 of *Gunnlaugs saga ormstungu*, Gunnlaugr ormstunga came upon two men fencing who were surrounded by many spectators. Gunnlaugr walked away in silence when he realized they mocked him as they fought.

Not everyone in the sagas is depicted as being skilled with arms. In chapter 24 of *Finnboga saga ramma*, Uxi struck at Finnbogi rammi (the mighty) three times with a two-handed axe, and three times failed to connect.

In chapter 24 of *Bjarnar saga Hítdœlakappa*, Þórðr Kolbeinsson sent the brothers Beinir and Högni armed with axes to kill Björn Hítdœlakappi at his home at Hólmr, on the shore of Hítarvatn.

When they made their attack, Björn used no weapons on the brothers, but he was able to grapple with them and bind their hands behind their backs. Björn then stuck their axes under their bonds in back and sent the brothers back to Þórðr, thoroughly humiliated.

Nor is everyone in the sagas depicted as being courageous in their use of weapons. In chapter 39 of *Harðar saga*, Þórólfr starri (stiff) entered Refr Þorsteinsson's house at night to kill him. As Þórólfr waited by Refr's bed-closet in the dark, his nerve failed him. Refr's mother, Þorbjörg Grímkelsdóttir, saw the killer and shouted a warning. Þorbjörg grabbed Þórólfr, got him underneath her, and killed him by biting through his throat.

Men were not above using dirty tricks to gain the advantage in a fight. In chapter 23 of *Fóstbrœðra saga*, Falgeirr Þórdísarson and Þormóðr Bersason were fighting on a cliff above the sea. Both had been severely wounded, and both were exhausted. While grappling, they fell into the sea. In the water, Þormóðr pulled down Falgeirr's trousers so he couldn't swim, and Falgeirr drowned.

Norman archers are illustrated on the Bayeux tapestry.

12

OTHER OFFENSIVE WEAPONS
IN THE VIKING AGE

THERE are a number of other offensive weapons mentioned in the sagas that are unknown today. Gunnarr's *atgeirr*, Egill's *kesja*, and Hrútr's *bryntröll* are known only by the description of their use in the sagas. No examples are known to have survived from the Viking age, and so these weapons remain mysterious.

Even seemingly well known weapons, such as Gunnarr's *bogi* (bow), have an element of mystery. First, we'll look at what is well known about these weapons and then consider some of the more speculative aspects.

Bows were used primarily for hunting, but they were also used in battle in situations where men desired to target their opponents from a long distance away. In mass battles, archers opened the action before the opposing sides moved forward to fight at close range.

Bows were made from a single piece of the wood of a yew (*Taxus baccata*), although ash, or elm wood were also used.

Based on surviving fragments, it is thought that bows were between 160 and 200 cm (60 to 80 in) long. Very few complete Viking-age bows are known to have survived, so any estimate of the length, construction details, draw weight, or range is highly speculative.

A complete bow found in Hedeby was made of the wood from a yew. It is 191 cm (75 in) long and generally oval in cross section, about 40 by 33 mm (1.6 by 1.3 in) near the center of the bow and tapering toward the ends. The nocks, which hold the bowstring at the ends of the bow, are grooves cut into the wood of the bow.

Pictorial evidence suggests that shorter bows may have been used in the Viking era. The bows shown in the Bayeux tapestry seem to be considerably shorter than the height of the archers, although medieval illustrations of this sort have to be used with care. Size and spatial relationships are often distorted in these images.

Arrowheads were made from iron and are found in a variety of shapes and sizes. Historical arrowheads from Iceland are shown on the next page. Arrowheads are not commonly found in the graves of warriors because bows were mainly used for hunting. In Iceland, arrowheads have been found in only two pagan Viking-age graves. Many more arrowheads have been found at house sites, including the three arrowheads shown in the sketch, which range in length from 10 to 15 cm (4 to 6 in).

Arrowheads had a tang that was driven into the shaft and secured with cordage and pitch or resin. A few socketed arrowheads have been found, in which the shaft fits into a socket in the head.

Although evidence is slight, shafts may have been as long as 70 cm (28 in), and perhaps as

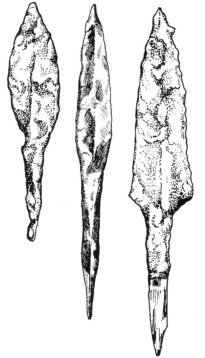

Above left: A reenactor demonstrates a replica Viking-age longbow. Above right: Pictorial evidence suggesting shorter bows, such as this archer illustrated on the Bayeux tapestry, has to be used with caution. Left: These three Viking-age arrowheads were found in Iceland. The longest is 15 cm (6 in) long. Arrowheads are rarely found in the graves of warriors, since bows were used mainly for hunting. (*Illustration: Michéle Hayeur-Smith, Fornleifastofnun Íslands*) Opposite above: Using his bow, Gunnarr single-handedly defended his home at Hlíðarendi in south Iceland, shown as it appears today. Gunnarr killed or wounded ten of the attackers before his bow string was cut.

large as 10 mm (3/8 in) in diameter. Hardwood shafts were used to secure the tang of the arrowhead firmly. A complete Viking-age hunting arrow found at Oppdal in Norway is 69 cm (27 in) long overall, and the birch shaft is 8 mm (0.3 in) in diameter at its widest.

The estimated draw weight of one 10th-century bow is 90 lbs (40 kilograms-force), and the effective range of this weapon is estimated to be about 200 m (650 ft), but any estimates have to be considered highly speculative given the dearth of evidence.

Medieval Icelandic law, however, gives a different estimate of range. The distance of the flight of an arrow, *ördrag* (bowshot), was a unit of measure commonly used in Icelandic law. For example, *Grágás*, the medieval Icelandic law book, requires that the court empowered to confiscate an outlaw's property be held within a bowshot of the outlaw's home. A later addition to *Grágás* defines the bowshot to be 200 *faðmar* (about 480 m, or 1600 ft). Perhaps the maximum range, rather than effective range, was used when writing the law.

It seems likely that archers used bows with draw weights to fit their capabilities, so there must have been some variation in the draw weights of bows. After the bow of Einarr þambarskelfir (string-shaker) was broken at the battle at Svölðr, as told in chapter 108 of *Ólafs saga Tryggvasonar*, King Óláfr Tryggvason threw him his own bow, telling Einarr to continue to shoot. Einarr fitted an arrow, and unaccustomed to the king's light bow, drew the head behind the bow. "Too weak, too weak is the king's bow." He threw the bow aside and took up his sword and shield.

Perhaps the most notable use of a bow in the sagas is Gunnarr Hámundarson's single-handed defense of his home at Hlíðarendi against an attack led by Gizurr hvíti (the white), as told in chapter 77 of *Brennu-Njáls saga*. From a loft in the upper level of the house, Gunnarr used his bow to kill or wound ten of his opponents before his bow string was cut by one of the attackers.

In the battle on the ice at Vigrafjörður described in chapter 45 of *Eyrbyggja saga*, the

Top: At the battle on the frozen Vigrafjörður in west Iceland, archers shot at men who had climbed on rocks to get better footing. Bottom: In naval battles, arrows were shot between ships. During the battle at Svölðr, King Óláfr shot most often with his bow, but sometimes threw spears. (*Otto Sinding, Slaget ved Svolder, 1883–84, Photo © O. Væring Eftf. AS*)

sons of Þorbrandr took a defensive position on a rock jutting above the ice, where they had good footing. Steinþórr Þorláksson and his men had a hard time on the ice against such a strong defense. Two Norwegians with Steinþórr ran a short distance across the ice to where they could shoot arrows at those on the rocks, making things very dangerous for Þorbrandr's sons.

The fjord is shown as it looks today in the photograph on this page. The saga says that

Snorri goði's shepherd watched the battle from the rock cliff at the extreme left edge of the photo, then ran back to the farm at Helgafell to get help.

Bows were used in naval battles. Once engaged, men on opposing ships shot arrows and threw projectiles from one ship to the other, attempting to clear the decks of men so that the ship could be taken. Chapters 106–111 of *Óláfs saga Tryggvasonar* describe the sea battle in

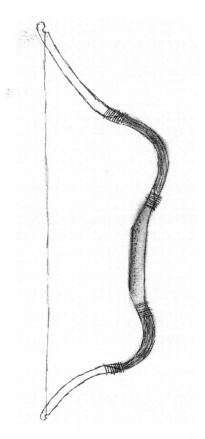

Above left: An 8th-century carving on an Anglo-Saxon casket shows a Saxon archer with a longbow. Below left: A Chinese silk painting, dating from the Viking age, shows a Chinese archer with a short composite bow. Did Vikings use composite recurve bows? Above right: A composite bow is made from a number of different materials, rather than from a single piece of wood. A recurve bow curves away from the archer when unstrung.

which King Óláfr Tryggvason died, which took place at Svölðr in the year 1000.

King Óláfr was onboard his ship, *Ormr inn langi* (*The Long Serpent*). The saga says the king shot most often with his bow, but sometimes he threw spears (*gaflak*).

With him was Einarr þambarskelfir, described as the best shot anywhere. Einarr fired two close shots at Earl Eiríkr, before Eiríkr's bowman, Finnr, fired an arrow that hit Einarr's bow. With Einarr's next shot, his bow broke. King Óláfr asked, "What cracked with such a loud noise?"

Einarr replied, "Norway out of your hands, king."

As with other weapons, bows were used to threaten. Before the battle at Svölðr, Úlfr rauði, one of King Óláfr's men onboard *Ormr inn langi*, questioned the king's command, implying cowardice on the part of the king. Óláfr fitted an

Gunnarr and his brothers were ambushed near the shore of the Eystri-Rangá river in south Iceland and fought near this stone, now known as Gunnarssteinn. Evidence found near this stone may suggest the use of composite recurve bows in Viking times.

arrow to the bow in his hand and aimed it at Úlfr, who said, "Shoot in another direction, king, where the need is greater."

Even a Viking-age weapon as well known as the bow has an element of mystery. Available evidence suggests that only longbows, made from a single piece of wood, were used in Viking lands, similar to the reproduction longbow shown earlier, and similar to the longbows used by other northern and western European people in the Viking age.

However, some intriguing but speculative evidence suggests that recurve composite bows similar to those used in eastern Europe and Asia may have been used in Viking lands. A sketch of an eastern composite bow is shown on the previous page, along with a contemporary illustration of a Chinese archer with a composite bow from a Chinese silk painting that dates from the Viking age.

A *composite* bow is made from a number of different materials, rather than from a single piece of wood, like a longbow. A *recurve* bow curves away from the archer when unstrung, but toward the archer when strung.

Eastern bows were composite and recurve. They were made from wood, sinew, and horn or bone. Bows made in this manner store more energy for a given bow length. Thus a short recurve bow has a range nearly as great as that of a longbow, offering advantages to archers in situations where the longer bow would be troublesome, such as in dense forests or on horseback. Some historical eastern bows are asymmetric, with the upper limb longer than the lower. The Icelanders referred to this kind of bow as a *hún-bogi* (Hunnish bow).

Konungs skuggsjá (*The King's Mirror*), a 13th-century Norwegian training manual, refers to a *horn-bogi* (horn bow) in chapter 38, calling it a useful weapon for a mounted warrior because it is easy to draw while horseback. The hornbogi may refer to a composite húnbogi, made partially of horn.

Similarly, a horn bow (*hornboga*) is mentioned in *Beowulf*, the old English epic poem that dates from the Viking age. In chapter 34, Hæðcyn killed his brother Herebeald with an arrow shot from a *hornboga*.

Are these references to composite eastern style bows, partially made from horn? The reference in *Konungs skuggsjá* would seem to be because it specifically mentions one of the known benefits of an eastern bow.

It's been suggested that the reference in *Beowulf* refers to the nocks at the tips of the bow around which the bowstring was looped and that were made of horn in some historical periods. This suggestion seems unlikely. Although archaeological evidence is sparse, it does not appear that horn nocks were in use in Viking times. The nock was made in the wood of the bow.

If these literary references to horn bows are actually references to eastern-style composite bows, it would suggest the possibility that composite bows were known in Viking lands. Eastern Europeans, such as the Magyars, were using them during this period in history, and it's possible that some of their enemies to the west, such as the Carolingians, used them, too. Is there any evidence that suggests Vikings used composite bows?

The tortuous trail of evidence that suggests this possibility begins in chapter 63 of *Brennu-Njáls saga*. Gunnarr Hámundarson and his brothers Kolskeggr and Hjörtr Hámundarson were ambushed by Starkaðr Barkarson and a much larger band of men. The brothers were able to kill fourteen of the ambushers, while of the brothers, only Hjörtr was killed.

The battle took place on the shore of the Eystri-Rangá river, near the large stone known as Gunnarssteinn (Gunnar's stone).

In the 19th century, erosion brought to light several graves above the river, a short distance from Gunnarssteinn. The grave sites are on the right in the photo on the facing page, on the far side of the road across from the stone.

One of graves contained a decorated ring made of bone. The ring is fairly large, about 3.8

During the Viking age, nocks on the bow around which the bowstring was looped were probably made in the wood, as shown on this modern replica.

cm (1.5 in) in diameter. It seems too big to be a finger ring, but too small to be a bracelet.

Although the skeletal remains in the grave were not complete, the ring was found adjacent to the distal end of the radius and ulna, where the hand would have been located had the hand bones survived.

Interestingly, the ring was decorated with images of harts (stags). The name *Hjörtr* means *hart*. Did the ring belong to Hjörtr? Is it Hjörtr who was buried in this grave immediately adjacent to the battle site? The evidence is not convincing, but it is an intriguing coincidence.

Archaeologists have speculated further on this find, suggesting that the ring is a thumb ring of the type used by eastern European bowmen to protect their thumbs while using a composite bow. The draw weight of the eastern

Above: One of the graves found near Gunnarssteinn contained this decorated bone ring. (*Þjóðminjasafn Íslands*) Below: The ring was decorated with images of harts. Was this the ring of Hjörtr, whose name means hart and who was killed in the ambush on this site? (*Illustration: Michéle Hayeur-Smith, Fornleifastofnun Íslands*)

composite bows can be substantially over 100 lbs (45 kilograms-force) and perhaps as much as 150 lbs (70 kilograms-force). These bows were drawn with the string hooked in the thumb, which was hooked under the knuckle of the first finger. The string rested on the ring, which protected the thumb. The use of this kind of draw with this kind of ring is well documented in eastern European and Asian lands.

Combining all these speculative elements together, it has been suggested that the bone ring from Gunnarssteinn is an archer's thumb ring belonging to Hjörtr, implying that Hjörtr used an eastern-style thumb draw and further implying that he used an eastern-style composite bow, which suggests that his brother Gunnarr, Iceland's most celebrated archer, may have used one as well, suggesting that composite bows may have been known and used in other Viking lands.

It's certainly plausible that Icelanders and other Viking people came in contact with this kind of bow on trading voyages to eastern Europe and Asia, or in service with the Varangian Guard in Constantinople during the Viking age.

Yet a great deal of evidence contradicts this highly speculative conclusion. Surviving eastern thumb rings have a different shape than the bone ring found at Gunnarssteinn, with characteristic features missing from this ring. Generally, the eastern rings have a projecting tongue that lays on the ball of the thumb, protecting it from the string. However, some later Chinese thumb rings share the simple cylindrical form of the ring found at Gunnarssteinn.

The saga says that Hjörtr was carried home by Gunnarr on his shield and buried there, rather than at the battle site. If home means Gunnar's home at Hlíðarendi, it is no small distance (about 12 km, or 7 mi) from the battle site where the ring and skeletal remains were found.

Last, even if an archer did use a thumb ring and a thumb draw, it scarcely proves that his bow was an eastern-style composite bow.

Although the available evidence is tantalizing, I believe it is too scant to support the conclusion that eastern bows were used by Vikings. Perhaps more supporting evidence will come to light in the future.

The saga says that Hjörtr was taken home and buried there, probably to Gunnarr's farm at Hlíðarendi, shown as it appears today.

A number of weapons are mentioned in the sagas that are unknown from other sources. Surviving examples of these weapons from the Viking age are not known to exist, although one wonders if there is an unrecognized lump of rusty iron in some museum's storage locker that was once one of these weapons. The old Icelandic words for these weapons are translated differently by different sources.

The *atgeirr* was Gunnarr Hámundarson's preferred weapon in *Brennu-Njáls saga* and is usually translated as *halberd*, although sometimes as *bill* or *javelin*. In addition to using it as a weapon, Gunnarr routinely vaulted onto the back of his horse using his atgeirr. The saga text suggests that the weapon could be used for thrusting and cutting.

A memorable use of the atgeirr appears in chapter 77 of *Brennu-Njáls saga*. Gizurr hvíti and his supporters gathered outside of Gunnarr's home at night in preparation for an attack. They weren't sure if Gunnarr was at home, so they sent Þorgrímr to find out. He climbed the outside of the house to the roof. Gunnarr was pre-

pared, having been awoken by the death cries of his dog, killed by the attackers in an unsuccessful attempt to prevent the animal from raising an alarm. As Þorgrímr passed by a window, Gunnarr thrust at Þorgrímr with his atgeirr. Þorgrímr fell off the house and returned to where the attackers waited. They asked if Gunnarr was at home. Þorgrímr replied, "That's for you to find out, but I know his atgeirr is at home," and he fell dead.

However, it's unlikely that Gunnarr's weapon was a halberd. Halberds came into prominence in the 14th and 15th centuries. They are long-hafted pole weapons topped with an axe, a hook, and a spike.

From the way Gunnarr uses his atgeirr in the saga, one wonders if it might have been like a *glaive*, a pole weapon used in the later Middle Ages.

Gunnarr's atgeirr is thought to lie at the bottom of Breiðafjörður off the point of land called Skor in west Iceland, lost in a shipwreck in the 18th century.

Egill Skalla-Grímsson used a *kesja* on several occasions, such as in chapter 57 of *Egils saga*, and

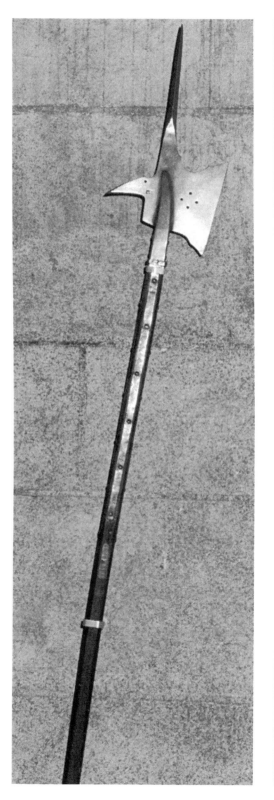

Opposite left: Gunnar's atgeirr is sometimes interpreted to be a halberd. This 16th-century halberd is in the collection of the Higgins Armory Museum. Opposite right: It is possible that Gunnar's atgeirr was more like a glaive. Three 16th-century glaives from the collection of Higgins Armory Museum are shown. Above, Gunnar's atgeirr is thought to have been lost in a shipwreck off of the point of land known as Skor in west Iceland.

usually translated as *halberd*. In chapter 2 of *Gísla saga*, Gísli Súrsson used a *höggspjót*, also translated as *halberd*. One source suggests that atgeirr, kesja, and höggspjót all refer to the same weapon, but it's unknown what it might have been.

In chapter 66 of *Grettis saga*, a giant used a *fleinn* against Grettir Ásmundarson, usually translated as *pike*. The weapon is also called a *heftisax*, a word not otherwise known in the saga literature. The saga says that the weapon had a wooden shaft and was equally suited for cutting or thrusting. That description makes it unlikely that the weapon resembled a pike, which is useful only for thrusting.

In chapter 30 of *Harðar saga*, Hörðr Grímkelsson threw a *gaflak* (javelin) at a man, killing him. In chapter 53 of *Egils saga*, there is a detailed description of a *brynþvari* (mail scraper), usually translated as *halberd*. It had a rectangular blade two ells (1 m, or 40 in) long, but the wooden shaft measured only a hand's length. The word *bryntröll* (mail troll) also appears in the stories, translated as *halberd*. In chapter 37 of *Laxdæla saga*, Hrútr Herjólfsson struck Eldgrímr between the shoulders with a bryntröll, splitting his mail and cutting through Eldgrímr's body.

So little is known of the *brynklungr* (mail bramble) that it is usually translated merely as *weapon*. Similarly, *sviða* is sometimes translated as *sword* and sometimes as *halberd*. In chapter 58 of *Eyrbyggja saga*, Þórir Gull-Harðarson threw his sviða at Óspakr Kjallaksson, hitting him in the leg. Óspakr pulled the weapon out of the wound and threw it back, killing another man.

Rocks were often used as projectiles in a fight. These effective and readily available weapons discouraged one's opponents from closing the distance to fight with conventional weapons.

Other improvised weapons were called into service in a fight. Steinþórr chose to retreat to the rockslide at Geirvör prior to a fight, shown as it appears today, so that his men would have a ready supply of stones to throw at their opponents.

Prior to the battle described in chapter 44 of *Eyrbyggja saga*, Steinþórr Þorláksson chose to retreat to the rockslide on the hill at Geirvör, where his men would have a ready supply of stones to throw down at Snorri goði and his men.

In chapter 11 of *Kjalnesinga saga*, Búi Andriðsson was ambushed by Helgi and Vakr Angrímsson and ten other men on the hill called Orrostuhóll (battle hill). Búi climbed the hill and carried some stones with him. From the higher ground, he threw the stones to keep his opponents at bay. By the time Búi's supply of stones ran out, he had killed four of his ambushers.

Everyday items were sometimes called into service as weapons, according to the sagas. A variety of mundane items were used in fights, sometimes with lethal results, including a boathook (*Hávarðar saga Ísfirðings* chapter 4); a whale bone (*Hávarðar saga Ísfirðings* chapter 10); a scythe (*Finnboga saga ramma* chapter 40); a pitchfork (*Finnboga saga ramma* chapter 32); a clothes beater (*Reykdæla saga og Víga-Skútu* chapter 22); a boat oar (*Víga-Glúms saga* chapter 27); mane shears, used for trimming a horse's mane (*Bjarnar saga Hítdælakappa* chapter 32); and a sled runner (*Eyrbyggja saga* chapter 37).

13

THE END OF THE VIKING AGE

THERE is no single event that signals the end of the Viking age. The Viking people didn't die off, nor were they conquered or killed; rather, they continued to live on their lands in Scandinavian countries, in the North Atlantic settlements, and at their new homes in other European lands.

The Viking age came to an end when these people stopped their Viking raids. The raids no longer turned the profits that they once had, so these entrepreneurial people turned away from raiding, while they continued their profitable trading voyages. There were several factors that contributed to the end of regular raiding by the Viking peoples.

Through the Viking age, many European lands grew from having weak or no central authority to becoming countries ruled by kings having strong central authority. These central authorities raised trained, standing armies capable of mounting effective defenses against Viking attacks, defenses that were weak or absent at the beginning of the Viking age.

In addition, these central authorities began to defend the more desirable targets with permanent troops, and by altering the physical structures at the sites. Defensible towers were built at towns and monasteries where valuables and people could be moved quickly in the event of a raid. Some monasteries were moved inland,

away from the reach of ship-based Vikings. The island monastery at Iona in the Hebrides was raided three times by Vikings, in the years 795, 802, and 806. Beginning in the year 807, the monastery was moved about 35 km (20 mi) inland for safety.

Taken together, these changes meant that Viking raids were no longer profitable to the same degree they once were. Additionally, the Viking raids were not in keeping with some of the tenets of the Christian church, which had been adopted over virtually all of the Viking lands by the end of the Viking age. The arrival of the church in Viking lands and the decline of raiding are closely tied.

After two years of successful raiding east of Sweden, the Icelander Björn Hítdœlakappi visited the Christian King Óláfr inn helgi of Norway. It was shortly after Iceland had converted to Christianity, but at a time when some heathen practices were still being followed. The king told Björn that he wanted him to give up raiding, as is told in chapter 9 of *Bjarnar saga Hítdœlakappa*. The king warned Björn, "Though you think well of it, God's laws are often disturbed."

During the tenure of Bishop Gizurr Ísleifsson in Iceland at the end of the 11th century, after the close of the Viking age, the practice of bearing arms in Iceland was largely abandoned,

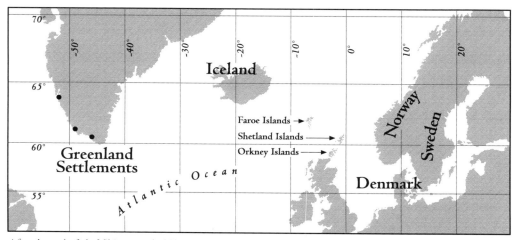

After the end of the Viking age, the Viking people continued living in their homelands and their North Atlantic settlements.

a significant change from the centuries before and the ones that followed.

The year 1066 is frequently used as a convenient marker for the end of the Viking age. In that year, at the Battle of Stamford Bridge, the Norwegian King Haraldr harðráði was repulsed and killed as he attempted to reclaim a portion of England. It was the last major Viking incursion into Europe.

GLOSSARY

aventail	A curtain of mail suspended from the helmet that protects the neck.
baldric	A belt over the shoulder used to suspend the sword and scabbard.
bind	A state of engagement where combatants' weapons are in contact. A bind can also be executed against the opponent's body using weapon components that don't cut, such as a shield or an axe haft.
boss	A domed, round metal component at the center of the shield which provides protection to the hand holding the shield.
buckler	A small shield, more commonly used after the end of the Viking age.
chape	A decorative and protective element at the tip of the scabbard.
crossguard	A protective metal bar placed between the grip and the blade of a sword, at a right angle to the blade.
eye	The hole in the axe head through which the haft passes.
falchion	A single-edged long knife used after the Viking age.
fuller	A central depression, usually placed in the middle on both sides of a sword blade, resulting in a lighter blade without sacrificing strength.
gambeson	A padded protective garment worn under mail.
grip	Also known as the haft, this is the portion of the hilt normally grasped by the swordsman.
guard	A standardized position from which to begin an encounter.
handwork	The action of an exchange after the swords have engaged.
hilt	The part of the sword excluding the blade, which includes the pommel, cross-guard, and grip.
inside	In describing the direction of a combat technique, a place inside of the space in front of the combatant's body and closer to the line of engagement. In an attack, a combatant desires to bring his weapon inside his opponent's defense, so there is nothing between the attacking weapon and the opponent's body.
inside shield ward	A defensive posture with the shield placed to the inside, nominally to the right for a right-handed combatant holding his shield in his left hand..

line of attack	The planned or actual trajectory of the weapon towards its target.
line of engagement	The imaginary line that connects the two combatants at the torso.
long edge	The "front" edge of a double-edged blade, in line with the knuckles.
messer	A single-edged long knife used after the Viking age.
onset	The initial attack of an exchange, begun from a distance.
outside	In describing the direction of a combat technique, a place outside of the space in front of the combatant's body and further away from the line of engagement.
outside shield ward	A defensive posture with the shield placed to the outside, nominally to the left for a right-handed combatant holding his shield in his left hand.
parry	A generic term for a defense against an incoming attack. A parry may merely stop the attack, or it may deflect the attack, or ideally, it may simultaneously counterattack.
pommel	The decorative weight at hilt end of the sword, which balances the sword and can be used for striking or wrenching.
running off	A deceiving technique for the sword in which the sword is rotated about the hilt.
scabbard	The protective case for carrying a sword on the body, usually made of leather and wood.
shield bind	A defensive technique in which the shield is used to bind the opponent's weapons and body.
short edge	The "back" edge of a double-edged blade, away from the knuckles.
tang	The narrow part of the blade extending through the grip.
target	A small shield, more commonly used after the end of the Viking age.
upper guard	A bar of metal at the end of the grip away from the blade. In early Viking swords, the tang attached to the upper grip.
winding	A technique for the sword in which a combatant rotates his blade around his opponent's blade to get past his opponent's defense in preparation for a follow-up attack.
withdrawal	An attempt to disengage from an exchange without being struck by the opponent.

SELECTED REFERENCES

On this page are listed some of the more useful references that are available and are recommended to the interested reader. Many more references were used to create these chapters.

I have listed materials here that are useful for a general reader, rather than for a specialist. I've tried to avoid listing materials that, in my opinion, fall short in scholarship or readability.

HISTORY AND GENERAL COVERAGE

Almgren, Bertil et al.: *The Viking*. Crescent Books, 1975.

Byock, Jesse: *Viking Age Iceland*. Penguin, 2001.

Foote, P.G. et al.: *The Viking Achievement*. Sidgwick & Jackson, 1970.

Graham-Campbell, James, et al.: *Cultural Atlas of the Viking World*. Facts on File, 1994.

Haywood, John: *The Penguin Historical Atlas of the Vikings*. Penguin, 1995.

Jón Jóhannesson: *Íslendinga Saga (A History of the Old Icelandic Commonwealth)*, Haraldur Bessaon, tr. University of Manitoba Press, 1974.

Page, R.I.: *Chronicles of the Vikings*. University of Toronto Press, 1995.

Pulsiano, Phillip, ed.: *Medieval Scandinavia: An Encyclopedia*. Garland Publishing, Inc. 1993.

Roesdahl, Else, et al., eds.: *From Viking to Crusader: The Scandinavians and Europe 800-1200*. Rizzoli, 1992.

Roesdahl, Else: *The Vikings*. Penguin, 1998.

Sawyer, Peter, ed. *The Oxford Illustrated History of the Vikings*. Oxford University Press, 1997.

WEAPONS AND TECHNIQUES

Forgeng, Jeffrey L. *The Medieval Art of Swordsmanship: A Facsimile and Translation of Europe's Oldest Personal Combat Treatise Royal Armouries MS I.33*. The Chivalry Bookshelf, 2003.

Hand, Stephen and Paul Wagner: "Talhoffer's Sword and Duelling Shield as a Model for Reconstructing Early Medieval Sword and Shield Technique." *Spada Anthology of Swordsmanship*, Chivalry Bookshelf, 2002, pp. 72-86.

Kristján Eldjárn, *Kuml og haugfé*, Mál og menning, 2000.

Meyer, Joachim: *The Art of Combat*, Jeffrey L. Forgeng, tr. Greenhill Books, 2006.

Oakeshott, Ewart: *Records of the Medieval Sword*. Boydell, 1991.

Peirce, Ian G.: *Swords of the Viking Age*. Boydell, 2002.

Short, William R.: "Arms and Combat in *Sagas of Icelanders*," Hurstwic, http://www.hurstwic.org/library/arms_in_sagas/arms_in_sagas.pdf (accessed June 26, 2007).

Talhoffer, Hans: *Medieval Combat*, Mark Rector, tr. Greenhill Books, 2000.

SOCIETY AND CULTURE

Dennis, Andrew, et al., tr.: *Laws of Early Iceland: Grágás*. University of Manitoba Press, volume 1: 1980; volume 2: 2000.

Jochens, Jenny: *Women in Old Norse Society*. Cornell University Press, 1995.

Sigurður Nordal, *Icelandic Culture*, Vilhjálmur T. Bjarnar, tr. Cornell University Library, 1990.

LANGUAGE AND LITERATURE

Translations

Dronke, Ursula, tr.: *The Poetic Edda*. Clarendon Press, Volume 1: 1969; Volume 2; 1997.

Faulkes, Anthony, tr.: Sturluson, Snorri: *Edda*. Everyman, 1987.

Hermann Pálsson and Paul Edwards, tr.: *The Book of Settlements: Landnámabók*. University of Manitoba Press, 2006.

Larrington, Carolyne, tr.: *Poetic Edda*. Oxford University Press, 1996.

Viðar Hreinsson, ed.: *The Complete Sagas of Icelanders*. Leifur Eiriksson Publishing, 1997.

Literature references

Gísli Sigurðsson and Vésteinn Ólason, ed.: *The Manuscripts of Iceland*. Árni Magnússon Institute in Iceland, 2004.

Jónas Kristjánsson: *Eddas and Sagas*. Hið íslenska bókmenntafélag, 1997.

McTurk, Rory, ed.: *A Companion to Old Norse-Icelandic Literature and Culture*. Blackwell Publishing, 2005.

Vésteinn Ólason: *Dialogues with the Viking Age*. Heimskringla, 1998.

Religion and Mythology

Lindow, John: *Norse Mythology*. Oxford University Press, 2001.

Simek, Rudolf: *Dictionary of Northern Mythology*, Angela Hall, tr. D. S. Brewer, 1993.

Turville-Petre, E.O.G.: *Myth and Religion of the North - The Religion of Ancient Scandinavia*. Holt, Rinehart, and Winston, 1964.

SHIPS

Crumlin-Pedersen, Ole, ed.: *Aspects of Maritime Scandinavia AD 200-1200*. The Viking Ship Museum in Roskilde, 1991.

Crumlin-Pedersen, Ole and Olaf Olsen, ed.: *The Skuldelev Ships I*. The Viking Ship Museum in Roskilde, 2002.

INDEX